To Sonja

Patty A Wilson

Pennsylvania's
Lost Treasures
True Stories of
Treasures
Yet To Be Reclaimed

Piney Creek Press

Copyright © Patty A. Wilson, 2013

Published by
Piney Creek Press
PO Box 227
Roaring Spring, PA 16673
www.ghostsrus.com

Printed in the United States of America

10 9 8 7 6 5 4 3 2 1

FIRST EDITION

Cover Design by Thomas Straub
Interior Design by Patty A. Wilson and Scott Crownover

Library of Congress Cataloging-in-Publication Data

Wilson, Patty A.
    Pennsylvania Lost Treasures
1st ed.

ISBN: 978-0-9700650-5-6 51499

1. History--Pennsylvania. 2. Folklore--Pennsylvania 3. Lost Treasures--Pennsylvania

Dedication

To my sons Daniel, Michael and Benjamin who are my treasures. May the adventure, mystery and intrigue of this world never stop inspiring all of you. And to Luke, my newest treasure of all. God placed you here to dazzle us with your brilliance and light. May we all have many adventures together-- my family and me.

Acknowledgements

This book could not have been written without the help of my readers and friends. I want to acknowledge Scott Crownover who is always there in so many ways to help. He willingly does research, listens to my tales and gives good advice. He also helps with many of the technical aspects of each book. From occasionally designing a cover to editing and layout, Scott's help and advice is truly appreciated. It is a joy to work with him.

A special thank you goes to James Andrews who made this book possible. Thank you my friend.

Contents

ALTOONA'S LOST GOLD
(Blair County)

By the beginning of 1861, the entire south-central part of Pennsylvania was in an uproar. General Lee was bringing the war to the north and Pennsylvania was feeling the sting of battle. Until this point the ravages of war were the exclusive domain of southern families, but now the folks of Pennsylvania were worried about being burned out, looted and killed. In order to protect themselves, local militias were mustered where the very young and the very old attempted to protect their homes and towns. On Brumbaugh Mountain in Bedford County, a fortified works was built to protect the Morrison's Cove area. There was also a fortified area in McKee, Blair County with the same aim, to stop the Southerners from marching into Altoona and taking over the massive railroad there. Such an incident would destroy rail transport, disrupt supply lines, and certainly could have turned the tide of the war.

Altoona, railroad capital of the world, is today a shell of its former self. Though it is a nice little city, it was once a bustling center of commerce. The railroad and the shops that serviced the cars and industry that sprang up in the area made this a very desirable target for General Lee. The bankers of the area well understood this, and they feared that the six banks that operated in Altoona would also be a target. They had heard of what had happened in other places when the Confederates had ridden in and looted banks, burned buildings and robbed the people. Of course, this was also happening all through the south, but at that moment folks in Altoona had more immediate concerns.

The bankers got together and decided to safeguard the money and to not allow it to fall into the hands of the Confederates. The Confederates used the money to buy weapons from the British, so the bankers needed to move the gold elsewhere. A plan was hit upon and soon set in motion.

The bankers each procured and filled a barrel with the gold and valuables from their banks. The six barrels were placed upon a wagon and the wagon was to go to Clearfield.

Arrangements had been made with banks in Clearfield for the gold and wealth to be secured there.

The bankers decided upon a more circular route than the one usually taken over Snow Shoe Mountain. Even today, Snow Shoe Mountain is noted for its steep incline and it was felt that the horses would not be able to pull the heavily laden wagon over such an incline. Therefore, the route became a more circular one northeast of Wingate, and then over the lesser incline of a smaller mountain.

Atop of the mountain stood the Mountain House Inn, where the men and their cargo would spend the night. The Mountain House was a popular inn and tavern and despite the importance of their work, the men decided to relax a bit and imbibe freely. They felt that if they paid too much attention to the supposed cargo of "liquor" they said that they were carrying, they'd cast attention upon themselves.

However, someone must have spoken out of turn, for as the men inside the building got ever drunker, the barrels were off-loaded one by one and rolled away. Now was no easy task! A barrel of gold would weigh tons.

In the morning, the men returned to the stables to hitch their horses and found that the wagon was empty. The panic was immediate! Who could have stolen the gold and where could they have taken it?

Through an investigation, it was determined that no other wagons had come into the stable or stable yard that night. Whoever the culprits were, they had apparently moved the gold by hand. That meant that it could not be very far away. It was postulated that the gold had to be buried somewhere in the area.

Despite the best efforts of both the police and a bevy of treasure hunters throughout the years, not one trace of the six barrels of gold has ever been found. The police believe that none of it has ever surfaced. At the time it was believed that whoever had hidden it had been prevented from returning for some reason and that the gold is still buried near the Mountain House Inn.

In 1960, a man by the name of Michael Furl claimed to have learned the whereabouts of the gold from his own parents who had learned it from theirs and so on. At that time, however, the government confiscated all gold and Furl saw no reason to tell since he could not keep the gold or be re-reimbursed for it. He died in Russville a year later still swearing that he knew where the gold was but he refused to tell. Since then, no one has come forward despite the fact that the U.S. Government no longer claims all gold as its own.

BOWMAN'S HILL

(Bucks County)

Late 1600's

Dr. Bowman sat down heavily upon his favorite chair in the parlour of his home on Bowman's Hill. He was not feeling well. He felt tired and his chest hurt. He had been dosing himself with his own special remedy for heart ailments, but the draughts were no longer helping the thundering in his chest. He felt his heart skip a few beats. In one way he was very tired and wanted the pain to end, but in another way he was not ready to die.

The rapid skip jump beating of his heart finally eased as he laid his head back and rested. His mind drifted as he closed his eyes. He knew that his time was short. He wondered who would find him? He hoped that it would be someone who liked him. Perhaps the woman who came to do the cleaning would discover his body and cover him up. He liked Mrs. Jenkins quite well. He hoped that when he died it would be Mrs. Jenkins who found him. He wondered if they would tear apart his house, dig up his grounds and look for the fortune that he had? The famous Captain Kidd fortune...

It had been a long time since Dr. Bowman had thought of his past and what had transpired to bring him to his home, but tonight it seemed like the veil between the past and the present was somehow very thin and he could see back in time.

It had been long ago when he was a young man that he had first met William Kidd. Kidd was a romantic figure to a young man that had just graduated from medical school. He met him and listened to the man's exploits upon the seas. Kidd was a privateer, a pirate who robbed the enemy at sea. Through time, Dr. Bowman had become more and more an intimate of Kidd's. The world called William by his romantic name of Captain Kidd, but to Dr. Bowman Kidd would always be his friend William.

He had been looking for adventure when he had first sailed with Kidd, but soon the money, the fighting, and all that it entailed captured him. Dr. Bowman was more than an employee of William Kidd's, he was a compatriot.

Dr. Bowman remembered how he had laughed when he heard at first that Captain Kidd had been captured. How many times had William cheated the hangman and had laughed about it? However, this time Dr. Bowman realized it was much more serious. This time their wealthy friends turned their backs on William. He had robbed too many British ships, had killed to many innocent people. Knowing an outlaw was no longer exciting. The new world was becoming civilized and men like Kidd were being driven out by the law. Money alone could not buy back Kidd's freedom and, eventually, Dr. Bowman learned that his friend had been dangled from a hangman's gibbet.

It was then that Dr. Bowman realized that he would have to change his life. Too many people knew that he was an intimate of Captain Kidd's. Bowman had his medical degree, his intellect and the money that he had amassed as one of Captain Kidd's men to fall back on. He would have to change his life completely and become respectable.

Dr. Bowman made his good-byes to Philadelphia and began his journey to find a large piece of ground. He finally decided upon an area now known as Bucks County. There he found a parcel of land that he particularly liked. He had contracted to have his home built there upon a hill overlooking his holdings. The hill came to bear his name and he became a businessman. Through the years rumors began to surface that Dr. Bowman had once been part of Captain Kidd's crew. Dr. Bowman neither denied nor confirmed the rumors. He likewise, did not confirm the rumors that he had amassed a vast fortune from his pirate days. However, he never seemed to hurt for money and he never invested money in a bank.

A pain suddenly shook Dr. Bowman again and he

winced. He opened his eyes and pushed the pain away. He needed to rest. He wanted to lie down. He made his way carefully to his room. He slowly changed into his dressing gown and laid down. For some reason there was no need to hurry.

He thought once more of his fortune buried on Bowman's hill. The rumors didn't tell the half of it he thought smiling. There was gold, jewelry and silver in the chest. He felt the great pain as it first tore at his chest. He would wonder no more if anyone would find the treasure. He had left Bowman's Hill and the chest behind forever.

It is believed that Dr. John Bowman was an intimate of William Kidd, aka Captain Kidd. His wealth was always attributed to his work with Captain Kidd. When Dr. Bowman died, it was believed that a vast fortune would be found. However, to this date no fortune has ever been found.

Today Bowman's Hill is part of Washington Crossing State Park in Buck's County. The legacy and legend of Dr. John Bowman has faded with time, but perhaps out there somewhere there is still a fortune waiting to be discovered.

THE NOTORIOUS ANN CARSON

(Philadelphia County & Northumberland County)

Ann was a beautiful young woman when she first met her sea captain, John Carson, in 1808. Ann was approximately half the age of the retired U.S. Navy Captain Carson. The early years of their marriage are a bit vague. But after several years of marriage, Captain Carson came out of retirement to take up a commission as Captain of the *Ganges,* which was sailing for China.

After the first year, Ann heard nothing from her traveling husband and she began to worry that his ship was lost at sea. During the next four years, Ann would come to believe that her husband was lost at sea and would not be returning. She lived her life as best she could in that state of limbo. For a woman of that time period, her social and financial status were in doubt. Though no record remains of her finances, she must have been worried about them because she was eventually forced to take in a boarder.

The person that Mrs. Carson rented a room to was Lieutenant Richard Smith of the 23rd Infantry Regiment. Smith was only slightly older than Mrs. Carson, and he was both handsome and very wealthy. In fact, he was the heir to the $1,000,000 fortune of his uncle Daniel Clark of New Orleans. A beautiful, lonely young woman and a dashing young military officer sharing the same house were a bad combination. The young couple soon fell madly in love. They did not announce their situation to anyone until Ann could have her husband declared dead.

However, fate was about to intervene. After nearly five years, Captain Carson suddenly arrived home.

The young lovers were shocked and horrified to see the Captain. The old man was unremorseful for his long absence and ready to claim his conjugal rights. However, Ann was not as ready to grant him such rights. In the following weeks, there grew a terribly tense situation in which Captain Carson discovered that his beautiful young wife now had a lover and no longer wanted anything to do with him. Amazingly, Captain Carson did not insist that Lieutenant Smith move out of his home.

However, one night the two men were alone in the parlour when they began to argue over Ann and the situation. Exactly how the situation progressed would never be known, but the result of the argument would forever change the lives of John, Ann and Lieutenant Smith. Smith pulled a gun and shot Carson dead.

Philadelphia was rocked by the scandal. Alderman Binns, a local newspaper editor and a former friend of Ann Carson's, would be the man to hear the case against Lieutenant Smith. He would bind Smith over for trial along with Ann Carson. His friendship with Ann would not sway him.

The trial that followed would bare Ann's life to public scandal and she would find that polite society had shut its door to her forever. However, Ann was not overly grieved by the social outcasting. She was fighting for her life and the life of her lover. The verdict of the trial would set Ann upon a course that would end her life in a strange and tragic way. She was acquitted of any guilt in the death of her husband, however, her lover, Lieutenant Smith was found guilty. He was sentenced to hang.

Ann desperately loved the young Lieutenant and she went to her old friend, Alderman Binns, and begged him to contact his dear friend, Governor Snyder. She pleaded for Binns to ask Governor Snyder for a pardon for Smith. Binns was infuriated with Ann for her wantonness and for her continued support of Smith. He not only refused to speak upon Smith's behalf, but he would write a scathing editorial about Ann and the possibility of a Governor's pardon.

Ann was infuriated with Binns and in desperation she came up with a plan that would give her revenge against Binns and would save her beloved as well. She would kidnap Alderman Binns and hold him until Governor Snyder signed a pardon for Smith. Unfortunately, Binns always surrounded himself with a cadre of acquaintances and Ann and her two employees, Henry Way and "Lige" Brown could not ever get him alone.

Ann sunk further and further by the day. She was infuriated by her inability to capture Binns, and so she decided to attempt to kidnap his son, but Binns learned of her plan and kept his son under guard.

Ann then decided to kidnap the Governor and force him to sign the pardon in order to save his life. On one of her visits to Smith, Ann confided a new plan to go to Selinsgrove to the Governor's home and take his son. Smith would then confide the plan to one of his cousins, but the cousin would double cross the couple and sold the information to Binns who got word to Governor Snyder.

Governor Snyder then signed a warrant for the arrest of Ann Carson and her "gang."

Ann and her hired thugs were hurting for money and at Lancaster, Henry Way decided to rob a drover. However, the drover fought back and captured Henry Way.

Ann and Lige continued on and made it as far as Clark's Ferry before they were captured while renting a room at a small boarding house. The local militia arrested Ann and Lige and she was left in jail on $5,000 bail. She was taken to Harrisburg to await trial.

While Ann was in prison in Harrisburg, word came to her that Lieutenant Smith had been hanged. Her efforts were for nothing. Her destruction did not even grant her the life of heart's desire. Now she had only to survive.

Eventually Ann's friends raised the bond and she was released. Ann disappeared for a while and during that time she took up various illegal activities to support herself. She moved away from the more populated areas of Philadelphia, Harrisburg and Lancaster. She settled in Northampton County. There she formed up a gang and began rustling cattle and committing robberies. She next turedn her hand to the more lucrative trade of counterfeiting. The way counterfeiting worked was that she became a "front man" for a gang of counterfeiters. She would be given bogus money and then would pass it in exchange for real money in stores and banks.

Ann used her looks to good advantage. She was still a very beautiful woman and she could look and act the part of a lady. Ann chose the guise of a beautiful Quakeress and she dressed the part. She would pass bogus money in that guise and did quite well. It is believed that she amassed a great fortune in gold and silver through her nefarious occupations. Ann met and joined up with the king of Pennsylvania bandits, David Lewis. The couple, along with her real life lover, Fred, traveled the east coast passing money for some time.

Ann obviously didn't trust banks and couldn't just waltz into a local bank and tuck away her amassed money. After all, a poor Quakeress would not be able to explain where such a fortune had come from. It is believed that Ann hid her portion of the money upon her homestead. She is believed to have buried it near her home.

Eventually, Ann would be recaptured while trying to pass bad money at the Girard bank. She would be convicted of counterfeiting and was sentenced to serve her time at the Walnut Street prison. Here Ann would be assigned to work in the infirmary. She was said to have been a good and kind nurse. In fact, she redeemed herself by working with the typhoid victims when the fever swept the prison. Ann worked in the infirmary until she passed away from typhoid herself on April 27, 1824.

It is believed that her fortune was never recovered. Indeed, she refused to talk about it while in prison. Ann Carson would leave this world a decent, loving woman and also one of the most notorious female criminals to have ever traveled Pennsylvania. It could be argued that much of her fate was sealed by the times. A genteel woman could not get a "real" job, and so Ann had been forced to rent out a room in her home when her uncaring husband abandoned her. Falling in love was only a natural thing for a young woman to do, and no one could have foreseen what was about to befall her. Ann chose an unconventional path and one that would make her famous, but her life was filled with romance, tragedy and possibly a treasure that still is waiting to be found.

COLUMBUS BROWN'S DREAM

(Venango County)

1883

Columbus Brown found himself walking through a forest and along a stream. It was like no forest he had ever seen. It was thick and the tree tops shut out the light. He would have believed that it was twilight if not for the bright light that briefly flickered when the breeze stirred the tops of the trees. The water burbled and murmured along and he felt compelled to follow the water. It was as if someone else were guiding his steps along the water's edge. The water turned around a bend and he knew that whatever was there was what he needed to see.

It was quiet. It was too quiet. He felt a certain fear, but he could not identify to himself why he felt this fear. Where were the people? Where were the animals?

Ahead of him he heard a noise and he slowed down. It sounded like someone shouting. He had just wished for such a noise, but now his heart shuddered at the sound of the voice in the distance. Something was wrong with it. He couldn't understand the words even though the voice was clear and loud.

His mind scrambled to make sense of the sounds. The voice was speaking in a foreign language. It sounded like ... French!

Columbus came to the edge of the clearing and stood in the shadows. He was merely one more waving silhouette in the dappled sun that shone upon the field before him. Beyond the field there was a fort. The water led to the fort. As he looked around, Columbus recognized some things. He recognized the lay of the land and the mountains beyond that. He was at the mouth of French Creek, but what he could not understand was the fort. There was no fort there.

Columbus Brown felt that he must be still. He watched life moving around the fort. Men in their blue and yellow uniforms moved around. The uniforms were shabby and ragged as if they had much use.

He saw a group of men come from the fort and walk out into the field. With them was a man who was well dressed. Columbus took him for a commander or leader of some sort. Two of the men carried shovels and two more struggled with a small chest. It didn't make sense that a chest so small could be so heavy unless the chest was filled with something heavy like say, gold.

Columbus felt compelled to watch. It was as if he was meant to see this. He slipped behind a tree and slowly walked along the shadowy tree line closer to where the men were in the field. He kept the trees between himself and the field, but he knew that he had to get closer and see that box.

The men marched out into the field near a single tree and stopped. The two men with the box put it carefully down. A man unfolded a camp seat for the man in the fancy uniform. The men began to dig the dirt up near the tree.

Columbus watched carefully. He looked for landmarks and things that he could find later. The tree seemed like the most obvious thing to see. It was a half grown sapling that had a main trunk and two twisted branches on one side. On the other side there was a broken limb that pointed like a long finger in his direction. He thought that he would be able to remember that tree.

Suddenly, Columbus Brown was back in his bedroom. He startled awake as the box plunked into the ground. For a second he was disoriented. He struggled to tell reality from the dream. In the darkness of the early morning hours, he realized that it had all been a dream, but it was such a clear dream. There was something about the dream that he could not seem to let go of.

Throughout the morning, the dream haunted Columbus as he went about his work. He kept telling himself that it was just a dream, but for him it was so much more.

By early noon he could not tell himself it was just a dream anymore. He grabbed a shovel and started off. He was headed for French Creek and the site that he had seen in the dream.

He made it to the headwaters of French Creek, but it took him a little while to see the tree that he had seen the night before. It was bigger now, much older, but still he knew that it was the same tree. On one side there were the two twisted branches, but what he remembered the best was the long broken branch like a pointing finger. He just knew that it was the same tree. Now it was an old, mature tree but he remembered it clearly. He grabbed up the shovel and ran toward the tree.

As he sunk the shovel into the ground for the first time, he hoped that no one saw him. Not only because he didn't want to share his treasure if there was one, but also because if there was no treasure he was on a fool's errand.

Each time Columbus stopped to rest he called himself every kind of fool, and yet he picked up the shovel again and dug. At last the shovel struck something hard. He fell down on his stomach and reached in. His hands could not reach that far down. The hole had to be six feet deep. Columbus was forced to dig the hole larger so that he could get down into it to lift up the box. It took him all afternoon and well into the darkness, but he could not make himself stop.

At last he had the little box out. It was a heavy iron box almost three feet long and not quite two feet deep and two feet wide. He busted the rusty lock with the shovel and a rock. Inside he could not believe his eyes. Even in the failing light he could see that it was gold and silver coins.

By now Columbus was exhausted, but he needed to get the box back to his home. He carried it, dragged it and pulled it along. He would not leave that box. It was not all about the gold and silver, although it represented to him a life that he had never dared to dream of. It was as if this box was part of a mission that he had to complete.

In time, people would come to learn the incredible story of Columbus Brown. He would tell the story of the dream and display the iron box that he had dreamed of many times. The box had a tag on it on which was written M. Joincaire. M. Joincaire was once the commander at a fort called Fort McNeil which had been built by the French in the early 1700's. Columbus had found a box approximately three quarters full of coins that dated from 1724 through 1754. In 1882, the coins were valued at $27,000.00. It was a fortune for Columbus Brown.

Fort McNeil did sit at the head of the French Creek and a M. Joincaire was commander there. In 1749, Le Marquis de Vaudrevil, the French Royal Governor in America ordered Chabert Joincaire to build a series of 40 forts or outposts. When M. Joincaire and Le Marquis de Vaudrevel returned to France in 1756, they had fallen out of favor with the French government. They were tried for crimes against the crown and their series of forts were abandoned. Along with the chest, at each site a heavy lead plate declaring the land as French territory was also buried. If any of the plates could be found or the chest of gold and silver, they would be worth a small fortune.

The forts are dotted along the old Boone Road and along a road that M. Joincaire built from Coudersport to Warren. It is believed that spread between the forts is a fortune estimated to have been as much as $500,000.00 in the mid 1700s.

Other forts known to have been built by M. Joincaire were Fort. Presque Isle, Fort Venango and Fort le Boeuf. Most of the buried treasures were never recovered. In fact, the treasure that Columbus Brown found at Fort McNault was the only treasure known to have been recovered to date. That means that there are 39 treasure boxes still buried throughout that section of the state. Today there are old maps available to mark the trail that M. Joincaire took. Much of the ground is used today, but there are still large parcels that remain much has it had been when the gold was buried.

Why Columbus Brown was given his vision is unknown, but what is known is that it was a very accurate vision. His dream proved that there are treasures out there buried by the French military that were never recovered. Their value today cannot even be guessed at, but it might be worthwhile to study up on the French military's movements in the area. Remember that the gold was buried deep, and like Columbus, you'll have to work hard to unearth it again.

BURIED AT KINZUA

(McKean County)

It was a cold, rainy winter day in Emporium. Ice was forming a crust over the snow that was difficult to bust through. Most folks were going about their work or huddled close to their woodstove. It was one of those days when the chill of the weather just seemed to get beneath your clothes and make your bones ache. No one was expecting any excitement that winter's day in 1898. Emporium was not known for its exciting ways.

Perhaps it was the bad weather or sheer desperation that made the lone man walking down the slushy little street decide that today was the day for his plan. Perhaps the man was so desperate that he did not even have a plan, but simply reacted to his bad situation by doing something so outlandish that it shocked the little town. Whatever the reasons, the man veered into the bank as he pulled his hat low over his eyes and his handkerchief up over his nose and tied it from behind. He pulled an ancient gun from his coat pocket and an old flour sack from his other pocket. There was no one in the bank except the teller behind his little metal screen and a lady clattering at a typewriter in one corner.

"This is a robbery," the man hissed, shoving the flour sack at the startled teller as he waggled the gun in front of the teller's nose. "Give me all your money--I mean every penny you've got!" The harshness of the man's voice galvanized the teller for a moment. He knew that he had to appease this fellow or get shot. He glanced at the secretary at her typewriter and realized that no help would come from that quarter. He feared for both of their lives.

"Yes sir," the teller mumbled as he fumbled for the open end of the flour sack. Quickly he began emptying money into the bag. With the bank robber behind him, the man walked into the vault and began shoving the neat bundles of cash into the bag. The robber spotted bags of gold coins and pointed the gun in that direction.

"Those, too," he instructed menacingly.

"That's all there is," the bank teller told the robber. "Why don't you just leave now. There's no need to hurt anyone."

The bank robber pushed the teller into the vault hard so that the teller fell down. Then the robber turned upon his heel, hefted the bag laden with gold coins onto his back, vaulted over the railing between the isle way and the door, and was gone.

The bank teller scrambled to his feet and ran for the back door shouting that the bank had just been robbed. It only took the bank teller a few seconds to reach the constable's office and tell his story. The bank manager was found and told of his loss. Men began to gather to help track the thief.

The snow and rain were both a help and a hindrance. It certainly did slow down the bank robber and gave them a chance to track him, but it also slowed down the men who were tracking him. Darkness would fast be upon them, and so the men paused long enough to gather lanterns and torches. Certainly the bank robber would not have the benefit of light and that would be an advantage for the townsmen.

The men struggled through the growing gloom of twilight, following the footprints in the snow. In places they could see that the bank robber had stumbled into deep drifts up to his thighs and had been forced to set down the heavy sack of money in order to extricate himself. He certainly would be making precious little progress at that rate.

However, they came to an area where the man seemed to have disappeared. They could not tell if he had slid down on the hard ice crust and left no trail, or if he had crossed Kinzua Creek and thereby left no trail. There was even a chance that the man had chosen to walk up or down Kinzua Creek.

The townsmen looked up and down both sides of the creek in the freezing rain and sleet, but could find no place to pick up the trail. Their enthusiasm was quickly waning as the night grew even more bitter. If it got much colder, the bank robber would probably be found dead himself in a couple days.

At last the men turned back in defeat. They had lost the trail and the bank robber. The town had lost its money. The men needed to warm up and dry out.

The bank manager had taken the time to figure out exactly how much had been stolen from the bank and he had tallied up the sum of $50,000 in paper, gold and coin. It was quite a haul for the fellow--assuming that he survived long enough to spend any of it.

For several days the townsmen kept looking for the bank robber. They tramped the woods looking for a path, a trail or a hideout, but could not find any. At last they gave up. The money and the bank robber seemed to be gone.

That was until about a week later when word reached Emporium from Hazel Hurst that the bank robber was there. He had wandered in a couple days earlier, sick with pneumonia, near dead and without any money. As the man was taken into a local house to be cared for, the constable from Hazel Hurst had come to speak to the fellow. It seemed that the man knew that he was dying and he had wanted to come clean about what he had done. Upon his deathbed, he admitted that he was the robber of the Emporium Bank, and that he had buried the money in mason jars under a flat rock within sight of the Kinzua Bridge northeast of Kishequa. He could give no better description and within a few more moments he was beyond talking or facing punishment for his earthly crimes.

From that day forward, treasure seekers have tried to figure out exactly where the bank money had been buried. The value of those old coins would make the loot well worth searching for today. To collectors, the gold coins would each be worth a small fortune, and it is not impossible that some of the lesser coins of that era would now be worth hundreds or even thousands of times what their face value was. Unfortunately, the only directions left by the dying man were that he had buried it within sight of the Kinzua Bridge on the northeast side of

Kushequa.

Today the area where it is believed the thief buried the fortune is part of a state park. The area is just off Highway 6 northeast of Mt. Jewett. Since then, the Kinzua Bridge has collapsed. Somewhere out there a fortune remains. But remember to find out if you may dig or if you are breaking the law! You certainly don't want to be fined while looking for illicit loot!

JOHN BROWN'S HOARDE
(Crawford County)

There is probably no more controversial figure in Civil War history than John Brown. Religious zealot, madman, renegade, outlaw, or hero, were all words used in association with John Brown. He defied the United States government because he believed them to be involved in an illegal and immoral act. He held to his principals even when they cost him the lives of two of his sons, and his faith was not shaken, even until the moment of his death. He never wavered nor shirked his duty as he saw it. Today he would be called a madman, but the seeds of our founding fathers very well could have lain in John Brown who stood up for his beliefs with his very life. I personally might not have agreed with his tactics, but I do admire his resolve. He was right in what he believed. Slavery was an abomination and the men and women pressed into slavery were being treated to horrors we can not understand today. John Brown was a man who saw an injustice and was willing to raise his voice and his hand to help. However, there is much more to John Brown than that single event at Harper's Ferry, West Virginia.

John Brown came to Crawford County in 1826 with his first wife and his three little sons. He chose Crawford County because it had good land and was a place for a man to work hard and prosper. There was still plenty of game for hides and he desired to start up a leather tannery. John was a big, strapping man and he purchased a 400 acre farm near Guys Mills.

John built a large tannery that would eventually employ fifteen men. He made a good living working the tannery, selling timber and running his farm. However, at the age of 26, John Brown was already an outspoken Abolitionist. He had a secret room built in the tannery where he would hide slaves on the run. His tannery was a regular stop on the Underground Railroad. During that time John was amassing a small fortune and other abolitionists were also investing in John Brown and his work. He was becoming famous.

Several years would go by before his wife would die giving birth to their seventh child. Eventually, John would remarry a local woman named Mary Ann Day. She would give John thirteen children.

John was outspoken on the cause of slavery, but he was far from a raging madman. He worked hard and became part of his community. He started the local post office and became the first post master. He also began the Independent Congregational Society in 1832 because he felt that the six mile drive into Guys Mills to the nearest church was too long.

During those years of prosperity, John was believed to have amassed a great fortune in money that was to go to the Southern Cause if and when the time was right. He could not house the money in local banks for several reasons. He could not explain where it came from and he could not allow the exact amount to become known for he feared that Copperheads, Pro-slavery sympathizers in the North, would steal the money. Therefore, it is believed that John Brown buried the money on his property not far from the tannery.

Brown never spoke of the money, and it is known that he never seemed to have a great influx of cash to use for the cause. Local people believed that he was saving the money until he saw a real need for it.

In 1836, John Brown sold his tannery and moved on. At that time there was still no sign of the money. Years later people would claim that John Brown had left the money in the ground near the tannery until he felt that he really needed it. They did not believe that he ever came back for the money.

Brown stayed for a time in Chambersburg before the

raid on Harper's Ferry, but he is not known to have made a trip to Crawford County at that time.

There is a chance that the fortune John Brown amassed for the Cause of Freedom is still on the old tannery property long forgotten and still buried. If it is, however, it might be more than a little difficult to find.

After John Brown sold the property it became a cheese factory, a gristmill and later a jelly factory. However, the structure burned down in 1907. The ruins of the building are preserved by the John Brown Historical Association as an historical landmark.

The story of John Brown's hoard is a bit like the story of John Brown himself. Very exciting and every elusive. Perhaps there was a treasure but it is gone, or perhaps it never existed. It is an intriguing mystery surrounding a man who was no stranger to intrigue in his lifetime

DAVEY LEWIS
GENTLEMAN BANDIT
(Statewide)

Without a doubt, no one could dare broach the subject of lost treasure in Pennsylvania and totally ignore Davey Lewis. Lewis was a most prolific thief and counterfeiter, but because of his endearing qualities he became a celebrity of Pennsylvanians rather than a villain. It would not be an exaggeration to say that Lewis supposedly lost more treasure than most people could find in a lifetime of looking. This will undoubtedly be the largest chapter in the book and after you begin to read the wonderful stories of Davey Lewis, you'll understand why.

I will caution the reader, however, that the factual Davey Lewis stories and the mythical ones have merged at points. I've done the best I could to weed out the myths and keep only the historical facts, but when history and myth has been melded so seamlessly, it would be virtually impossible for me to say that I have completed my task.

David Lewis was most probably born on Bald Eagle

Creek only about a mile away from Bellefonte. His father was a surveyor and his mother, Jane, accompanied her husband, Lewis Lewis, on his journeys. Davey Lewis was born in approximately 1790 and he was the youngest of the eight children that Jane would bear with her first husband. (She would subsequently remarry twice more.) As her baby, Davey seems to have been doted upon, and certainly Jane proved her devotion to Davey time and again.

During the War of 1812, young Davey joined the army and became a wagon driver. His work took him up into Canada but Davey was not military material. He deserted and was caught. He was sentenced to be executed but his mother borrowed a horse from a friend who was a local judge and made an arduous ride to seek a pardon for her son. She obtained the pardon and spared Davey's life.

Soon after his mother spared his life, Davey began to travel and drifted into the company of con men and criminals in Vermont. Lewis became a card shark and robbed or fleeced both British and American soldiers until the end of the war. He would ply that trade for some time and was quite successful.

Lewis is often described as a fine specimen of a man. Six feet tall, broad shouldered and narrow at the waist. His strawberry blond hair gave away his Irish heritage. He was considered handsome and he had the manners of a gentleman. Lewis enjoyed fine clothes, good cigars, alcohol and beautiful women. Dressed as a gambler, he could enjoy them all.

It was in a jail in the upper Provinces of Caniday (Canada) where Lewis probably met Philander Noble, a short, fat man and the brains of a large counterfeiting ring who recognized in Davey a wonderful potential. At that time, creating script (paper money) was relatively easy. Each area printed its own script and so people were dealing with a vast variety of colors, sizes and print designs. This made it easy for a good forger to create credible script. The operation was really quite simple. Noble created fake script plates based on real script. A good quality paper was obtained and used to print up the fake money. Then Noble had a force of men and women passing the script. Those men and women would enter towns all across the US and Canada and purchase something small. Then they'd offer up a large script note. The shop keeper made change and that was how the money was "passed." Davey Lewis was a "face man" or "front" for the gang. He was the one who exchanged the worthless script for good money or gold. With his good looks, charm, and wit he was able to pass vast quantities of such script before he was caught. Lewis would once say that he had passed over $1000 in one trip alone. The gang had over a hundred men and women and among them were many "face men." That meant that a vast amount of real money and gold was being quickly amassed. However, the effect that it was having on the national economy was horrible. It was literally causing a depression. Shop keepers were growing afraid to take any money other than gold for fear that they'd end up with phony script. Though Noble's gang was very large, it was certainly not the only gang plying the trade of counterfeiting.

Lewis was a bit of a prankster who enjoyed one upping the law. It was his brash charm and wit that would make him more than a two-bit hood. Even Lewis would eventually be found out and he was arrested multiple times for counterfeiting, robbery and assorted petty crimes. Lewis hated to be confined but he was not a violent man. His experience during one arrest in Bedford shows much about his character. One evening in 1815, Lewis returned to Bedford and was arrested under suspicion that he had purchased a horse with counterfeit money. Lewis calmly denied the charges but showed no signs of arguing. Instead he sat down and drank and played cards with his very captors. It was only when the sheriff got a rope that Lewis reacted. Lewis managed to get a pistol and pulled it only when the sheriff asked for a rope to tie him up. Lewis told him that he'd shoot his own brother rather than to be tied. He did discharge the pistol but it misfired. He handed the gun to the sheriff and allowed himself to be led off to jail.

It was Lewis's hatred of confinement that probably was at the root of another part of the Lewis legend. It is said that no jail could hold him and indeed that seemed true. Lewis escaped from Bedford jail three times, from Chambersburg once and from every other jail that tried to hold him. He did three of six years he was sentenced to serve in the Eastern State Penitentiary. He was pardoned by Governor Findlay who would later regret his kindness when his political enemies used Lewis's pardon and subsequent crime spree against him.

There is little doubt that Davey Lewis was a colorful character. He was a handsome man who loved life well. He was a man who grew up poor and could relate to the common man. He often did kindnesses for those in need. He gave money to the poor on several occasions and, even when robbing someone, would not take their last dollar. It was reported that he'd return about ten dollars to his victims and tell them that he'd not have it said that he'd steal a man's last dollar. He was non-violent and victims of robbery often told authorities that it was Lewis who spoke on their behalf and refused to allow his accomplices to harm them. For those reasons many who knew Lewis would remain loyal to him until the end. They'd hide him, spy for him and lie for him.

Among the many legends of Davey Lewis is the story of his taking lodgings with a widow and finding that she was upset. She told him that in the morning the sheriff was coming to take her cow and that meant no milk or butter or the little money she earned with both. Lewis gave her the money and then waited to rob the sheriff. He got his money and more.

In Bedford, he freed everyone during one jail-break except for one man who had robbed a poor woman. He then jailed the warden and his family and left that robber to care for them through the night. Later Lewis would do something similar in Chambersburg. It was there that he volunteered to help look for himself when he met a posse of farmers out looking for the notorious Robber Lewis. Lewis asked them what they were doing and listened in amusement to the tales of the desperado Davey Lewis. The men seemed a bit confused by everything including a description of Lewis. Lewis then offered to help them look for the highwayman for a while. He stayed with the company for several miles and then took off. He sent word back to them that they had shared a walk with the notorious robber Lewis and asked them how they had liked him? Another time, Lewis decided not to rob a man who spoke well of him and who was honest. He revealed his identity before riding off and letting a very startled and lucky merchant behind. The daring and dash of this handsome young highwayman and counterfeiter amused the people. Lewis stories were talked about in many a bar, store and home in Pennsylvania.

Lewis amassed fortunes but lost them just as quickly. He rubbed elbows with Governors and judges and conmen and thieves. When he was in jail in Chambersburg, Governor Findlay came to visit him quietly. The reason was never known, but the proof of the Governor's visit was in the jailer's notes. It was the middle-class that wanted to bring an end to Lewis and his ilk. They were the ones robbed by his counterfeiting and his years as a highwayman. In the end, it would be those citizens who would themselves arrest Lewis repeatedly and who would bring about his demise.

David Lewis died in Bellefonte in the only jail that ever held him, and only then because he was gravely ill. Lewis and an accomplice were most probably ambushed by a posse of citizens-- some bent upon revenge for past events. His partner was shot repeatedly and died only hours later. Lewis was shot in the thigh and arm. He was taken to the Bellefonte jail where a doctor and minister tended him. He lingered for a few days but never gave a confession, never told where his fortunes were hidden if they were, and only spoke to the minister about the condition of his soul. He died on a hard prison mat rather than have his arm amputated. He reviled the idea of being a "one-armed man." Even while dying, Lewis was said to have shown strength, dignity and courage. He would be buried about a mile from where he was born. He had lived only about thirty years, but in his lifetime he spawned a plethora of legends. Perhaps the most enduring one is that Davey Lewis was Pennsylvania's gentleman bandit. Through the years his misdeeds have been forgotten, but his daring, cunning and grace have made him Pennsylvania's Robin Hood.

To the best of our ability to tell today, Davey Lewis seems to have led an ordinary life until after his court martial for desertion. At that time his mother and step-father were living in the Carlisle area. (Jane Lewis's second husband's name was Leathers and her third husband was Stevens.) It is said that Lewis hid his first ill-gotten gains on his family's farm near Carlisle. A search of the census and the history books would be needed to turn up the exact location of the farm at that time.

However, it is believed that he hid money there. He is also credited with having hidden gold money and other valuables west of Carlisle along the Conodoguinet Creek. Lewis was said to have his first "hide-out" in this area.

There has long been a legend in the Lewistown area that Davey Lewis hid a saddlebag filled with ten thousand dollars in gold behind some rocks while he was being chased after a particularly lucrative robbery. Lewis was supposedly forced to leave the area to hide out for a time before he dared return to retrieve his gold. Unfortunately for Lewis, when he did return to the area he could not find the landmarks he had remembered because a flood had swept through the area. The gold was never reclaimed to the best of anyone's knowledge, and folks believe that it might still be in the area. All that is known today about the location is that Lewis was heading south from Lewistown and that the gold was stashed along the banks of the Juniata River. It is also possible that the flood waters dislodged the saddle bag and pushed it further down stream.

Near Beaver Meadows in Carbon County, Davey was also said to have buried over ten thousand dollars in gold. There are few details available today about this supposed cache of gold coins.

Near Chickie's Creek in Lancaster County is an area known as Chickie's Rock. It is on that ridge that Davey Lewis did actually have a cave hide out. Stories have long circulated that he hid money or objects near the cave he used for a hide out. There is historical documentation that indicates that Davey Lewis did have a cave hide-out in this area.

Davey Lewis was also known to have had caves he lived in or hide-outs in the following areas: South Mountain west of Gettysburg, Doubling Gap west of Carlisle and at the Bedford Springs one mile south of Bedford. The caves listed above are historically accurate. Contemporary testimony and proof exists for the fact that Lewis inhabited all of the caves listed above. The cave at Bedford has always been rumored to have had gold hidden in it. Of all the legends of gold that still surround Lewis's name, perhaps the Bedford story is one of the best. It is known that Lewis did have money when he was in Bedford. Before one of his arrests he had over $1500 dollars in the

Bedford Bank. There was more money found on his person. Is it possible that Lewis was cautious enough to not want to risk it all in one place and hid some above Bedford? Who knows, but he certainly did spend time in that area and was clearly financially flush during that time period.

When Davey Lewis died in 1820, he had fallen on hard times. He and a partner named Conley had been hiding out in the Bellefonte area and had been raiding spring houses for food. They had also been robbing travelers and had broken into several homes in the weeks leading up to their arrest. It is now believed that Davey Lewis had lost all his money by then. But at that time, it was believed that he had hidden the money until the heat was off but never had time to retrieve it after his capture. Immediately after his death stories began to circulate that Lewis had intimated in prison that he had a fortune in gold hidden nearby. Supposedly he said, that he could see the fortune from his very jail cell, but that no one would ever find it because it was so well hidden. When Lewis died, he took the secret of what happened to the cache with him--if there is truth to the story.

"I DON'T BELIEVE IN BANKS."

(Somerset County)

1890

John Crouch stood up and wiped his brow. It was a warm afternoon and he had been working for quite some time. He sat down and picked up the jug of cool spring water that his oldest daughter had brought to him only a little while earlier. The water was kept cool in the crockery jug and it felt good sliding down his throat. He looked out across his fields as he sipped at the sweet water. It was going to be another good year, he thought as he laid down the jug and went back to work.

John Crouch was a very lucky man and he knew it. He lived about four miles from Hillsboro on a little farm he and his wife had purchased long ago. He was a wealthy man, but he did not want others to know of it.

John had grown up very poor and he believed in thrift. He also believed that a man should take care of things for himself. He made his family do with what they had and he never had believed in banks.

John finished work just as the sun began to sink behind the trees and he made his way into the barn. His oldest son was bedding down the animals and his daughter was carrying a heavy milk bucket into the house slowly so as not to waste precious milk.

The house was really no more than a large shack. John did not believe in needless frills. He fixed the holes when they let the wind through and he made sure that the stock was cared for, but his family had learned to cope with his miserly ways long ago. They kept only the second best crops; he sold the best that they had. They made due with the wood that he could not sell from the woodlot and the meats that he didn't sell when in town. No one would have known that John Crouch and his family were wealthy. Even his own family did not know how wealthy they really were.

John thought about the heavy crocks of coins he had buried all around the farm. He didn't believe in banks, and so he did what he had always done and had taken care of things for himself. He had buried crock after crock around the farm and each crock was filled with gold and silver coins.

After supper was over and the dishes were done, John walked out into the grove of trees behind his house. His wife and daughter struggled to complete their work only by the firelight because a kerosene lamp would be an extravagance and John would not tolerate the waste of money.

He looked back at the shack that he forced his family to live in and felt a sense of satisfaction. He walked to the barn and found the shovel in the darkness. He went back to the trees and sunk the shovel into the ground. The earth turned easily there along the edge of the field and he quickly unearthed a crock. Using only the moonlight, he quickly lifted the crock and opened it. Inside there were thousands of dollars in coins. He had several such crocks buried around the property. There were two in the fields and more near the barn and others elsewhere as well. In all he had over three hundred fifty thousand dollars buried, but

John wanted no one to know how much they had. His wife and daughters each got a new dress every year and he had patches on his breeches so they were fine.

He buried the crock again and walked back to the house. A low glow from the fireplace lighted his path as he made his way to the rope bed that he shared with his wife. Something had been nagging at his mind all evening long. He was worried.

While he had been in the field working that afternoon, the minister from Hillsboro and two of the men from the church had stopped to talk to him. They were looking for donations to build a new church and they had asked him for money to help with the endeavor.

John had turned them down flat and had threatened to throw them off the farm. It was then that one of the men had said something that was still worrying him. That man had shouted at him angrily, "Everyone knows that you've got money out here hidden, John Crouch, you old miser. You make your family suffer and beat yourself up working all hours not to pay a hired hand and yet you have money. We know what you get paid each year for your grain and horses. You never spend a penny, and so you probably have every penny you ever made hidden around this place somewhere. You ought to be ashamed of yourself that you can't even help with the Lord's work."

John had been furious because of how close to the truth the man had been. "You get out of here, now," he had shouted back. "Get out of here all of you or I'll go get my gun and then you'll see how freely I can spend my lead."

The men had left then at the urging of the minister, but John was shaken. What if folks in town really did know that he had his money hidden around the farm? What if they really did want some of it. He knew that his wife had long voiced her opinion that the money should be put in a bank, but banks get robbed and then folks would also know how much money he had. He couldn't risk either event happening.'

John fell into bed and pulled the blanket up over himself. Tomorrow he thought he might dig up his money and move it. But even that was a problem because he worried that someone would see him.

Something hit John in the leg and sent a burst of pain

through him, startling him awake. His wife seemed to scream at the same instant and he struggled up. The butt of a gun hit him as he got to his feet in the faint light of two kerosene lamps that had somehow been lit. John fell back to the floor.

A gruff voice hissed, "Don't kill him. He knows where the money is." That was when John lost consciousness.

The robbers gathered up the children and herded them into the living area where they had dragged John and his wife. Mrs. Crouch was holding her youngest child and comforting the child as he sobbed softly.

There were several of them, but Mrs. Crouch could not tell exactly how many. All she knew was that they were in terrible danger. The men wore rough cloth over their faces and carried guns. She could see their eyes above the masks but little else. A lifetime of living with John made her feel guilty and worried about the kerosene that the men were wasting. It was a fleeting, crazy thought but she could not help it.

One of the men stepped forward and she realized that he seemed to be the leader. "Tell us where the money is and we'll get out of here," he said pulling Mrs. Crouch up from the floor and tearing her ratty, thread bare nightgown.

Mrs. Crouch shook her head. "In there," she whispered pointing at the cabinet where John kept their money.

One of them began rifling through the cabinet and turned quickly shaking his head. "Nothing there," he hissed.

Quickly Mrs. Crouch hurried on. "In the flour bin. Feel around for a little jar. John hides the money in there."

The man pulled open the flour bin built into the side of the cabinet and plunged his filthy hand into the gray flour. He came up with a dusty jar and for a second they all seemed excited. However, when they opened it up and poured it out on the table they were disgusted. In it there was less than $10.00 that John kept for running the house.

"That ain't what I want," the leader said grabbing Mrs. Crouch's face and pulling it close to his own. Foul breath made her gag but she dared not show any emotion. She knew that they had to have some money around because John had just sold a couple calves but she didn't know where it was. She told them the truth.   Her main concern was for the children grouped together near the coals of the fireplace.

Then we wake up the old man, don't we?" the man growled at the fellow who had gun butted John Crouch. Someone picked up the water jug and poured it over John. He came around sputtering and found that his nightmare was real.

John tried to tell the men that his wife had given them all of the money that he had but they didn't believe him for an instant. They wanted money and they wanted it now.

When the bodies were found, the local police surmised that John Crouch did not give up his stash of money. He had seen his wife and children brutally slain, and then had died himself without revealing the whereabouts of his precious money.

They looked over his account book that he had kept locked carefully in a box and hidden under the floorboards near his bed. The book indicated that through his life he had amassed a fortune of over three hundred fifty thousand dollars, but that he had not spent the vast majority of the money. It could not be located in any bank within the state, and so it was surmised that the money was buried around the property. The fact that they could find no holes told the rest of the story for the police.

John Crouch had kept his fortune a secret for all of his life, and took the secret into eternity with him.

Through the years, people tried their luck at finding the fortune of the greedy man but the miser has protected his secrets well. A few small stashes of coins have been dug up through the years, but the vast majority of the money is still in the miser's custody on the ground where the farm used to sit. It may stay in the ground for eternity or someone might just dig it up one day but if they do, it is hard to tell how old John Crouch would react. He valued it more than his family and his own life, and he might value it still-- even from the grave.

THE GENERAL'S CACHE
(Somerset County)

General Washington looked back at his men stumbling through the deep snows and against the blowing winds. It was bitterly cold and they were struggling to carry along with them the equipment needed for war. The General realized that things were going badly for them. He was deeply troubled.

Ahead of him in a grove of trees his aides had set up his tent and the men began to make lean-tos, build fires and make other provisions for the night. A stringy cow had been purchased from a farmer earlier in the day by force and they had slaughtered it. He was grateful for the food for the men. Food and shelter were constant problems for the men in the Army. Now that they were struggling along the Laurel Highlands in the height of winter, matters had grown more drastic than ever. It was rapidly becoming a desperate situation.

The general huddled close to the fire in the little camp stove as he ate the choicest of the meat from the cow. It was tough and he had to cut it in little bits to get it down but he knew that matters would be much worse if they didn't do something soon.

The General knew that he would not be able to get his men and equipment through the mountains in the massive snows that had developed. He was faced with a choice that he didn't want to make. He would have to stash the weapons and unnecessary provisions and return for them later.

When the meager meal was over, he spoke to his aides about the situation. His orders were simple but depressing. He ordered them to pick a couple men to ride along the ridges and look for caves or likely areas where they could secure the heavy weapons until spring. Then he would have the men hide the materials there so that they did not fall into British hands, and he would hope that they could come back for them in the spring. Right now he knew that if he didn't leave them behind the men outside would not make it through the mountains.

When the word came that there were several caves along the ridge, Washington must have felt relief. His responsibilities were many and weighed greatly upon him. He had to get his men to a place where they could survive, but he could not risk allowing the weapons to fall into enemy hands.

The military implements were safely stashed and the front of the cave was secreted as much as possible. It was a great loss, but not as great a loss for the Army as the loss of men would be. Guns could be retrieved or replaced, but the men who made up the army were irreplaceable. Without them the guns would sit silent and the war would be over.

It is said that no one ever came back for the guns and equipment stashed there that winter day. The weapons and provisions are still sitting in a cave awaiting a brave soul to find them to this day. Some of the supplies will be rusted beyond recognition, but whatever can be found would be worth a fortune to collectors today, and it would be worth even more because of the association with General Washington. The very thought of finding cannons which Washington once had ordered fired is enough to bring collectors of Revolutionary memorabilia out. The historical significance of such a find, too, should be considered.

There are many caves in the Laurel Mountain Ridge of Somerset County, and they have become repositories for several treasures. According to some sources there are at least two other treasures secreted in those caves.

Several chests of silver and gold coins are said to have been secreted in a cave during the Civil War. The chests were supposedly part of a payroll for Union soldiers that never made it to the men. Others say that along with the treasure, the soldiers hid cannons and other guns in some of the caves up there. There have been reports that some small caches of weapons have been found in some of the caves, but the big treasures were not located --at least not yet.

DOANE'S GANG
(Bucks County)

The Revolutionary War bred any number of heroes, but it also spawned cowards, thieves and profiteers. Many of the young men who turned to robbery did so because they were trying to stay out of the Colonial Army. Some were British sympathizers who felt pressed to betray their country. Others became criminals to avoid serving in either army or the fines that came from shirking that duty.

The British were more than happy to have these rabble-rousers causing trouble in the Colonies. The thieves did much more damage to the American cause of Independence than they did to the British rule. In fact, the British paid such men to cause trouble.

In Plumstead Township in Bucks County, there lived a very pious family by the name of Doane (or Doan). The family belonged to a little religious order in the area and Israel Doane, the father of the clan, was a well-known and respected man. He was honest, upright and considered a good man by all. He and his wife raised six sons and that was when the trouble began.

The boys were led by the two oldest brothers, Joseph and Moses. Through the years, the boys gained a reputation for being great athletes, able horsemen, talented, and handsome. The boys were all well-built and broad shouldered. They were always favorites with the ladies for their looks and prospects. The boys were also excellent students with the careless regard that those naturally gifted with a good mind seem to have for study. With all of their looks, their family's reputation and their good minds, the boys could have had a sterling future. They were decidedly in the Tory camp as was their father, but that alone would not have destroyed their chances for a grand life.

However, the boys began to commit petty crimes. No one could ever pin the thefts upon the boys, and so they continued on. Joseph Doane became a school teacher in the area. Two of the other boys walked to Philadelphia where they joined the British Army. This would become an important factor in the coming crime spree. The Doane Gang found that the

British would buy all of the horses and livestock that they could purloin from their neighbors. Their brothers in the British Army became fences and arranged for the stolen animals to be sold to the British officers.

The boys who remained in Plumstead Township began targeting Whig families. They stole horses and livestock. They masked themselves and became highwaymen. They robbed homes and terrorized the neighborhood. Though rumors flew as the thefts continued, no one could ever pin the crimes upon the Doane boys.

Moses took over leadership of the boys and a fellow by the name of Robert Steele joined the gang. By all accounts, Steele was even worse than the Doane boys were.

One night they robbed the farm of a Mr. John Shaw who was a known Whig sympathizer. Mr. Shaw's home was not only robbed, but he was badly beaten by the boys. They were becoming more brutish by the day, but on this night their true colors would show through. They stole the livestock from Mr. Shaw's barn and rode out.

The gang was far from done with their night of raiding. They next went to the home of Mr. Joseph Grier and broke into his house. They attacked Mr. Grier for his beliefs and beat him badly, too. They abused some of his family while Mr. Grier was too injured to help, and then the gang looted the house. They again stole all of the livestock and rode off.

Their next stop on that night was at a tavern nearby. The tavern was run by an older fellow named Colonel Robert Robinson. Mr. Robinson had run to fat as the years had gone by and was now a very portly older man. The Doane Gang burst into the tavern after it had closed and began to drink. Colonel Robinson had already retired to bed but they found him and literally threw him down the stairs into the tavern to serve them. He fetched them food and drink and tried to retreat behind the bar, but the gang would have none of that. Colonel Robinson would also serve as their entertainment. The gang would treat him in an especially cruel manner.

They trussed up the old man like a hog with his arms and legs pulled back painfully. Then they cut his clothes off of him. They lifted the naked, old man up onto the table where they were feasting. While they ate they abused him horribly both verbally and physically. They stole the money from the tavern, and then relieved the barns of the livestock. They left behind a badly beaten old man and they rode on into the night. What they didn't know was that the valley had had enough.

Before their spree was done on the night when they robbed Shaw, Jacobson, and Robinson, they would also rob and beat several other people. The gang would continue on their spree until they crossed the border into Montgomery County.

After Mr. Shaw had been beaten and robbed, he sent his son to fetch help. The boy ran to the nearest farming settlement where a group of Mennonites lived. These peace loving people refused to raise a hand for fear that they would be targeted and because they were of a different faith than those now being tortured.

The boy ran on until he came to another farm and there he received help. Soon a group of men were gotten up and they went on the lookout for the gang, but they would not find them that night.

During the next few hours the Doane Gang realized that they had overstayed their welcome in the little valley of Plumstead. No longer could the local folks overlook the thefts as the youthful indiscretions of basically good young men. Now the boys were outlaws and were hated by nearly everyone in the valley.

The next morning the gang was spotted by the posse that had been raised by Shaw's son. The angry men rode in hot pursuit of the gang into the Skippack area. There they came close to ending the gang's thieving ways. The gang was forced to give up their horses and flee on foot.

There was some shooting and Joseph Doane was shot in the face. A bullet passed through his cheeks but did him no major damage. He was abandoned by his brothers as they scrambled to safety and Joseph was arrested.

Joseph was taken to the Newtown jail and held there. He was arraigned and began his wait for a trial. He heard the angry murmurings that they would capture the whole Doane gang. He realized how bad things would go for him and he effected an escape while he waited for the first day of his trial.

He fled Pennsylvania and hid in New Jersey.

By now the legend of the Doane Gang was cemented in the area's lore. Some folks still felt sorry for the boys and shook their heads in disbelief that the fine young men had come to such an end, but the law was clearly taking a dim view of their antics. The Federal Government put up an $800 dollar reward for the return of Joseph or the capture of any of his brothers--dead or alive!

The boys realized that they would not be safe anywhere on the eastern coast. Some of the boys split off from the gang. Joseph would run to Canada after the news of the reward reached him.

However, Moses, their leader, and two of the other boys stayed together. By now they had amassed a considerable fortune and they saw no reason to stop their thieving ways. It is estimated that they had over $100,000 dollars hidden in various places by that time. Moses and the boys thought that they'd just lay low for a while.

The boys decided that they'd stay in the wilderness and that in time the heat would die down. Then they'd come back out and things would be fine. They knew of an old fellow along the Tohickon Creek whom they thought they could trust. He was a bit of a drunk and they'd keep him supplied with liquor while they holed up in his little cabin. For some time the boys were fine at the cabin, but word leaked out locally that the old fellow had some very infamous houseguests. Eventually, word reached back into Plumstead Valley where their parents were and Mr. Shaw learned of their whereabouts. He immediately contacted a Colonel Hart and they got up a party of men to go and arrest the miscreants.

The party managed to sneak up on the little cabin. Colonel Hart argued that they should take the boys back alive and came up with a plan to do so. He and a few other men would sneak up to the cabin, kick in the door and take the boys with no shots fired.

Unfortunately, the Doane boys had other thoughts. When Colonel Hart kicked in the door, the boys grabbed their guns and began shooting. They managed to kill one of the party named Mr. Kennedy before retreating to the bedroom for the standoff.

In the confusion that followed, two of the boys managed to shinny out of a small window and take off into the woods. That left Moses by himself. He was perhaps the most honest and decent of the group and he decided to give himself up without anymore fighting.

He threw out his gun and waited for orders. Colonel Hart called for the young man to come out. Moses Doane was promptly shot in the back by one of the men in the arresting party. It would later be known that the man who shot him was once part of the gang and had killed Moses in order to protect his own identity.

The other boys would come to various bad ends. Levi and Abraham stayed together and were later caught in Chester County. They were tried for their crimes and hung on September 24, 1788 without revealing the whereabouts of their fortunes. The only thing returned to Plumstead township were their bodies which were taken back to their parents.

The remaining brothers stayed in hiding, but Joseph, attempted to get them pardons. His efforts created a good bit of excitement throughout the state. Many people who had known the boys in Plumstead Township felt that they should be given a second chance, but those who had been robbed and beaten were not nearly as lenient in their views. A controversy raged in the state, and the boys did not receive their pardons. They also could not return to their old stomping grounds to retrieve their loot. Ironically, they were penniless and forced to seek employment or starve.

In the fullness of time, the boys were each captured and tried. The rest of the boys served time in prison or were executed. Joseph went to jail in Canada for crimes up there, but he got off the easiest of all of the boys.

It is believed that to this day much of the boy's loot is still buried in the mountains of Plumstead township. At least three areas have been identified as places where they secreted stolen goods and gold from the British in exchange for the livestock that they stole.

One of their cronies was a fellow named Preston Rich and they used his farm as a hangout from time to time. It is believed that on that farm they buried a large bundle of gold and silver coins. The former farm was located on the Mechanicsville Road near Buckingham.

It is believed that Moses and his brothers had dug up a considerable part of the gold, silver and jewels they had stolen and had reburied them near the cabin on the Tohickon Creek near Plumbsteadville where they had hidden out. The cache was never recovered and it is believed to still be there today. The area where the cabin was located is not exactly known, but it is believed that it was in the area of the Stover Park Creek.

A stash of silver coins was said to have been buried by the brothers along the stone wall of an old potters field cemetery in old Philadelphia near the Schuykill River. There has never been any indication that this treasure was ever found.

The last known hideout of the boys was in the caves along the Delaware River near Point Pleasant. When the boys rode into their cave along the river, they had with them nearly $19,000 in gold coins. The money did not leave with them. Conjecture is that the boys buried the gold there in case they needed it for a quick getaway in the future.

Unfortunately for the boys, crime paid well but they never lived long enough to dig it up and spend it. It is said that Joseph outlived his brothers and that when he returned from Canada he could not find the gold. Some of the loot had been moved, in other places the land had changed, and he did not even know exactly where some of it had been buried because he had fled to Canada early on. So are there still caches of gold, silver and jewels from the Doane Gang out there in the mountains and valleys of Plumstead township? Very probably, but finding it would take research, perseverance, and luck.

BRADDOCK'S BOOTY
(Allegheny County)

Today most Pennsylvanians don't realize that much of this land that we call Penn's Woods was once owned by others long before King Charles paid off a debt by giving it to William

Penn. Before the first European set foot on this land, the ground was the property of the Iroquois Confederacy and was home to dozens of different nationalities of Natives. Parts of Pennsylvania were under strong French control and parts were even claimed by the Spanish and Dutch. America was certainly up for grabs and it was far from certain that it would be British territory. The French joined with several Native nations and fought desperately to hold onto their territory. They fought over every inch of their property before it was abandoned.

June, 1755

Major General Edward Braddock was one of the first British Generals to step foot on American soil. His goal was to take back Fort Duquesne from the French. At this time there was still a major struggle for North American soil. The loss of Fort Pitt was a major point of honor for the British, but it was much more than that. Whoever held the land, laid claim to the great riches around it and to the major waterways that joined there.

Major General Braddock's task was far from easy. He would have to bring 2,200 men through one hundred twelve miles of wilderness. But he would also have to cut a path 12 feet wide through which the weapons would be brought along. He would do so despite the fact that many of the supplies that he requisitioned did not arrive. Along with him he would take a young George Washington who was a Lt. Col. at the time.

Major General Braddock would decide at one point to split his forces. He would move forward with the main force of approximately 1,300 men. Behind Braddock would come a smaller force of about 800 men who would be bringing along the majority of the cannons, weapons, and other supplies. Along with the military supplies, Braddock carried a supply wagon filled with gold. The estimates range from between fifteen thousand to twenty-five thousand dollars in gold. Part of this was in a pay chest that was to go to the troops. Braddock had also brought along a significant portion of his personal fortune. The man that Major General Braddock chose to drive this wagon was beyond reproach and his orders were to not allow the fortune to fall into enemy hands at any costs.

What Major General Braddock did not know was that his progress toward the fort was not going unnoticed. The French knew that he was coming and they had laid a trap.

Fort Duquesne was under the command of Captain Pierre de Contrecoeur. He realized that his troops were far outnumbered, but he had set his trap. He would ambush Braddock at the ford of the Monongahela ten miles from the fort. Captain Pierre de Contrecoeur would have at his command 35 French officers, 72 regulars, 146 Canadians and 637 Indians.

On July 8th, the trap was sprung. The French launched an unconventional attack upon the British. What the British did not know was that their Indian scouts were actually French informants leading them into the trap.

The battle was quick and bloody for the British. The British formed into standard military columns for battle, but the French and Indians did not fight according to British rules. The French and Indians were hiding in the woods along the fringes of the battlefield and firing from behind trees rather than forming up into columns in the open to shoot at each other.

There was confusion and Braddock found himself having to bring in support for the vanguard that had taken massive casualties. Braddock tried desperately to hold his forces and mount an offensive but he was fighting a losing battle. As he fought, he had four horses shot from beneath him on that day. At last he received a devastating wound when a musket ball shattered his hip. It was a wound that would kill Braddock four days later.

During this battle, many other things also happened. It was at this time that the Indians began to believe that Washington was somehow protected or invincible. He had two horses shot from beneath him and his clothing was torn by no less than four musket balls, but he had not a single wound.

When the battle began, the driver of the pay chest wagon had turned and fled for fear that the wagon would be captured. The driver was known to have turned south back the way they had come. He had hoped to make it to Fort Burd. He realized that the gold was slowing him down and he chose to stop the wagon along the way and bury or hide the chests. he did not know then that Major General Braddock would never be back to recover the money.

The soldier did make it back to Fort Burd but he could not remember where along the way he left the chests. He thought that it might have been close to the battlefield. The soldier had witnessed terrible torture and suffered great fear that he, too, might fall to the Indians who tortured and killed their victims in terrible ways.

There is truth to the idea that Braddock did order some of his valuables hidden. Near Chalkhill, not far from Uniontown, some trunks were found in a cave. These trunks contained items that were definitively linked to Braddock. Among the items found were military supplies.

There are several theories as to what happened to the pay chest and other trunk. One is that the gold was dumped into one of the cannons and pushed over a cliff near Dunbar's Camp. Dunbar was one of the officers under Braddock's command.

Other people speculate that the chests were buried on the battlefield. They believe that Major General Braddock had kept the gold near to him until things went badly. It is believed that the reason why the chests were not recovered is because those who knew the burial spot were killed during the battle or died within days of the battle.

No one knows for sure what happened to that gold, but it is commonly believed that it has never been recovered. Indeed, the French knew of the existence of the gold because of their Indian scouts and they would have loved to have recovered the chests but there is no definitive proof that they ever did. There is a rumored account that they dug it up but there has never been any more confirmation for this tale than any of the others.

Through the years, there have been many other theories and stories surface. One is that the Natives did find the gold and asked that it be given to them as bounty for their sacrifices on the battlefield. The French granted the request, in part, because they were vastly outnumbered by the natives and needed their cooperation.

Another theory is that Braddock had ordered the gold wagon to turn around well before they were ambushed. Historian Edward Williams found documents concerning

Braddock's journey west. In the papers was a reference to ordering the "money tumbril back to Fort Cumberland" at Wills Creek (Today known as Cumberland, Maryland). However, the money does not seem to have been logged in to the books at Fort Cumberland.

According to Ceane O'Hanlin-Lincoln in *County Chronicles A vivid Collection Of Fayette County, Pennsylvania Histories*, during an interview with historian Bruce Egli, Vice-President of the Braddock Road Preservation Association, there was a box of money, but it was French money that was lost. According to Mr. Egli, the British burned Fort Duquesne and the French soldiers were forced to flee and according to the journal of one Frenchman, a box of French gold was buried because it could not be carried off. The journalist does not know if the British ever found the gold. Interestingly, no matter how the tale is told, gold was buried somewhere along the route or near the French fort and perhaps it was never found. However, Mrs. O'Hanlin-Lincoln also states that she has it on good authority that near Jumonville, a farmer unearthed some gold British coins of the right vintage to have been part of the Braddock treasure. This only leads one to believe that somewhere nearby the rest of the fortune still waits to be uncovered.

INCIDENT AT DENT'S RUN
(Elk County)
July 1863

The young Army Lieutenant looked back at the wagons swaying along slowly behind him and silently surveyed the area where they now were. It had been a long trip so far and honestly the Lieutenant was not feeling well. In fact, he was feeling decidedly sick. The Lieutenant fought off the illness that threatened him; he had to get the wagons he was escorting through. Though his detachment did not realize it, they were transporting a fortune in gold.

Ahead of him the guide named Connors continued his even pace. Connors seemed indefatigable but the Lieutenant had been sick quite often during this journey. He could not explain it, but he knew that the sickness was about to descend yet again.

The story of what had brought the young Lieutenant to this point was a long one. The Civil War was raging on and the Confederate raiders were making quite a dent in the gold supplies headed to the Philadelphia Mint to be made into coin to be used to pay the Union soldiers. Several large shipments of gold had already fallen into enemy hands where it could be used to buy weapons and supplies from the British. The United States Government was quite concerned about the losses, and so they had begun a system of shipping the gold northward from Wheeling, West Virginia surreptitiously. The government had decided to ship the gold up through the state of Pennsylvania in a long circular route that would have the shipments arriving from the north rather than directly from the south. That was what had brought the young Lieutenant to that point. He alone knew that each wagon in the small wagon train had a false bottom where gold bars were secreted. In total the young Lieutenant was caring twenty-six 50 lb. bars of gold that totaled two million dollars in today's market.

Suddenly the ground seemed to shift under the young Lieutenant and he pitched forward.

The next thing the Lieutenant knew was that he was terribly hungry and thirsty. He ached all over and he had a hard time sitting up. He called Connors over to him because he had to know that they were still on the right trail and how long he had been ill this time.

Connors stepped into the darkness of the tent and he stood there, hat in hand, waiting. "You sent for me, Sir?"

The Lieutenant nodded and struggled to sit up. "Where are we? How long have we been stopped?"

Connors dragged a gnarled hand across his face that was covered by a growth of beard. "We're just outside of St. Mary's in the upper part of the state, Lieutenant. You've been sick for four days now."

"I understand that you and my Sergeant took care of me. I was out of my head at some points, or so the Sergeant told me. I didn't say anything did I--while I was ill I mean?" The Lieutenant sagged back against the crude pillow made from his horse blanket.

"Sir, you didn't say nothing that I can think of, Sir. Just some rambling is all." Connors met the Lieutenant's cornflower gaze. Something about that look made the Lieutenant pause. Had he mentioned the gold that weighed so heavily upon his mind while he was ill?

The Lieutenant gained his strength within the next forty-eight hours, and soon he ordered the wagons hitched once more. The team resumed its journey northward. Connors informed the Lieutenant that they were going to soon be passing through the town of Driftwood as soon as they got off the narrow path called Dent's Run.

That is the last that was ever known of the wagon train. The ten men, the horses and mules, the wagons and the gold suddenly just were no longer there. It is known that they entered Dent's Run, but they never came out on the other side.

Two months passed before the story of the lost wagon train once more made news. Connors, the civilian guide, stumbled into Lock Haven, about fifty miles east of St. Mary's which was the last town that the convoy had passed through. The guide was bedraggled, sick and nearly raving. Connors was nearly starved to death and demanded sustenance before he began his horrible tale.

According to Connors, the wagon train made it well into Dent's Run before the small contingent was suddenly surrounded by a group of men with hoods over their heads. The hooded men were heavily armed and quickly shot the men guarding the wagons. Connors insisted that he had been shot, too and left for dead, but after the men had driven off with the wagons he had crawled a long way from the area for fear that the murderers would return to finish off the job.

Connors did have a partly healed bullet wound and he was emaciated and obviously starved for quite some time. He insisted that he had subsisted upon whatever he could find while he struggled to survive. He also said that during that entire two months he had been wandering the woods within that fifty-mile area.

Connors story was vague and at times it didn't exactly fit together and soon folks began to say that Connors was the mastermind of a Copperhead gang. Copperhead was the name applied to any southern sympathizer who lived in the north. Those southern sympathizers were often actively plotting to help the south through subterfuge and spying. Could it be that Connors was a Copperhead, and that he fronted a gang of such people in the St. Mary's area who had stolen the gold and done away with the Army men? It would be a question that never would be answered.

Connors was questioned at length about what had happened not only to the gold but also to the Army men. Eventually some mule bones, believed to be from the Army mules, were found in a swamp in Dent's Run. The bones would yield up possible proof that the men and animals were done away with. If that were the case, then where were the wagons and the gold?

The Army literally drafted Connors as a scout and moved him out west. Connors became an alcoholic and when he was drunk he would at times admit to being part of a plot to steal the gold. However, once he sobered up he'd always recant the story. No one would ever be able to piece together the truth of what happened with Connors and the gold.

The U.S. Army was not going to give up on its gold that easy. They hired Pinkerton Detectives to search for the gold. For years, the men from Pinkerton would make a trip west to question Connors. It was said that well into the twentieth century, Pinkerton Detectives would occasionally show up in the Dent's Run area looking for the gold, since no one had ever found it.

Today the locals in the Elk County area still tell the story of Dent's Run (St. Rt. 555), and folks still speculate about the incident that took place there.

Rumors and little tidbits have kept many a treasure tale alive, and the story of the Civil War gold at Dent's Run is no different. It has been known for some time that the wagons, the carcasses of several mules wearing Army harnesses, and even some human remains were found in the swamps at Dent's Run in 1865. There have long been stories that 2 1/2 bars of gold were found under a tree approximately four miles south of the spot where the wagons were discovered. We also know that a survey team discovered the bones of three to five men dispersed over the area of a spring at Bell's Branch of Dents Run in 1876. This area was approximately seven miles from where the wagons had been discovered.

The United States government has long believed that the gold was too heavy to carry and that it was hidden in the general area of Dent's Run to be retrieved later. However, the war was going badly for the southern cause and it was believed that the Copperheads never had the chance to return for their blood-soaked gold.

LUCY BARNE'S SECRET HOARD
(McKean County)

Lucy Barnes listened as a stagecoach came rumbling into the dooryard of the Halfway House Hotel and wiped her hands. She was a busy woman, but she had enough curiosity in her that she wanted to see the new passengers. Her world revolved around the Halfway House Hotel and her husband Joseph. Joseph had built the Halfway House above the town of Hazel Hurst in 1859, and by the mid-1860's the hotel had become the most popular hotel along the route that would one day become Highway 6.

Lucy watched the dusty, weary travelers tumbling from the coach and smiled. There were several wealthy businessmen among the group and that meant that there would be plenty of money flowing through the hotel that night. She was always glad to see those genteel folks with money stopping over at her place. She watched as Joseph stepped out and greeted the guests. He was a man who enjoyed the people and she enjoyed the security of knowing that with the people came wealth.

As the evening wore on, Lucy took care of business. Long after the last guest retired she sat up counting the day's take by lamplight. She controlled the purse strings in the family and she was a careful guardian of the wealth. She finished filling a pottery jug with the gold coins and tamped it shut. She poured wax over the cork and took the jug to the bedroom with her. In the morning she'd deposit it in the safest place she knew of and it was not in a bank!

Among the things that Lucy distrusted, banks ranked highly. They were prone to robbery, bankruptcy and other maladies that did not incline her favorably to them. She believed that her system of banking was much better suited to the safety of her money. She deposited it in a secret spot on the wooded hills above Halfway House.

Early the next morning Lucy picked up her jug of money and a shovel and started out. It was barely daylight and she liked that time of morning because most folks were sleeping then. She felt safer walking along with that jug of money tucked under her arm, knowing that very few other folks were stirring yet. This was a scene that her husband and others would witness many times.

Where exactly the many jugs of gold were buried was never known, but it is known that they are in the hillsides above Halfway House. Lucy not only did not trust banks, she never trusted her own family. When she died suddenly in 1866, she had never revealed the location of the family hoard.

For long years Joseph and other family members tried to find the gold coins but they had no luck. Later on the hotel was sold and repeatedly the story of the gold was told until it became a legend. That legend took on more credence when a new owner's son found an old twenty dollar gold coin dating from the 1850's in the spring. Even this, though, could have been just a lucky coincidence, however, four more times twenty dollar gold coins from that era have been found in the old spring. It is theorized that through the years the pottery jugs have burst and the gold coins have washed down into the spring. Since old Joseph Barnes never got to spend the fortune he had amassed, it still remains strewn upon the mountainsides above Halfway House for some intrepid soul to find.

THE LEGENDARY TREASURE OF
SNAKE-SPRING TOWNSHIP
(Bedford County)

Thomas Croyle looked up from his work and wiped his brow. He acknowledged the men who had entered his blacksmith shop with a nod and a smile, and went back to pounding the horseshoe he was shaping. He thrust the hot metal back into the red hot fire before plucking it out to beat upon it once more. The men behind him were Indians and they waited quietly knowing that Thomas had to get the shoe shaped before he could turn his attention to them. In the 1750's there were more Indians than whites in Bedford County, and many a white man would not have turned his back upon the natives, but Thomas Croyle was not one of them. Thomas knew these men well and trusted them. In fact, several of them were relatives of his wife, Judith. Croyle was now a part of her family, and often was hired to work for members of the tribe who needed silver worked into ornaments.

When he dropped the horseshoe into the bucket of cold water, a sizzle of steam went up and Croyle wiped his brow again. He turned toward his visitors and smiled. "Well, brothers what can I do for you? You bring me silver again?" He grinned broadly to hide the fact that he was most interested in the silver.

One of the men with a knot of feathers atop his head and black and red streaks painted across his face stepped forward. In English, which would have been the envy of many a white commoner he said, "We want more of those spangles and ear rings you made before and more silver for chains. We wish to go to trade soon and this will bring a good price." He lifted a heavy hide bag and placed it upon the worktable in the corner. The other three men with him did the same.

Croyle walked over and dumped out the bags onto the scarred, crude table. He had known the Indian people long enough to know that they did not value personal possessions the way whites did. This silver had been dug out to use for trading for supplies for the entire village. He would not have to keep it

50

separated.

The silver did not look like much in its raw state, but as Croyle fingered the rocks with the precious metal locked within them he longed to find some silver of his own. He had questioned Judith many times about the silver mine but she had always insisted that she did not know exactly where it was. She had told him that only a few of the men knew so that there was less chance that the whites would find it and take it from them. Croyle longed to get some of the silver for himself.

"Same percentage as before," he said scooting the raw sliver ore backward so that he could hoist his bulk up on the table.

"We know," said one of the men. "The arrangements last time were acceptable. How long will this take?" Croyle thought of the stories of Indians he had heard before coming here. These men were far from the simple savages he had expected. These were men of intellect, and with business instincts that they used to keep the village alive. Many of the people were multi-lingual, speaking several Native tongues as well as English, French and some Spanish. He had been quite impressed with Judith and her people when he had come to the area. He always enjoyed his visits with her people, but he knew that he was still an outsider. They gave him business and paid him well for turning the raw silver into trading material, but he was still white and they felt they could not trust him enough to show him where they found the precious metal.

"I'd like to send with you for some supplies, too. If you'd tell me where the silver is I'd work some up for myself and get some extra supplies in before winter comes. There are a few things Judith would really like." It was an old ploy and he knew it would not work.

"We do not mind sharing with you, Thomas, but as we have said before you must let us blindfold you. We will lead you to the silver and you may take whatever you can carry back here. Do you agree?" Judith's brother with the painted face raised his eyebrows in inquiry.

Thomas shrugged. Though he got along well with the Indians, he did not know that he would want to be led blindfolded anywhere by them. "Perhaps one day, but for now I have enough work to keep me busy." He nodded toward the rocks at his side. "One day, I shall take you up on it, but I'd better get back to work or I'll not have this lot ready for you when you go to trade." He jumped down and nodded toward the stone house where he knew well that Judith was watching them and hoping that he'd send her brothers over so that she could visit with them.

"Now I'd better get back to work, but you had better stop by the house before you fellas leave or Judith will never forgive me. She has made some things I'm sure she'll want you to take back."

Thomas watched only briefly as the five men trouped into his house. He saw Judith in the doorway in her favorite blue dress and he knew that she had hurried to change, because earlier she had been wearing an old calico print made from material he had brought back from Carlisle.

Late in the evening, Thomas walked in the house and sat down to rest his aching bones. Working raw silver into ornaments was hard work. The smell of pipe tobacco hung in the air vying with the aroma of rabbit cooking into a stew. Thomas had not been hunting in two days so he knew that one of Judith's brothers had brought them the meat as a gift. He sometimes thought it was a real pity that more folks didn't have the Indian ways. They were kind people in their own way.

"Dinner is ready," Judith said as she looked up from the fire. "Take off those dirty things and wash up. I'll have the biscuits ready in a moment." She turned back to finish her work and Thomas paused a moment just reminiscing about Judith. She was truly a beautiful sight to behold. How he loved her dark hair splayed out on the homespun of her night dresses, and how he loved her delicate, quick movements which reminded him of the colorful little humming birds which darted from flower to flower.

Judith was sitting the heavy pewter dishes on the table as he came back into the cabin. He had washed up and changed to a fresh shirt for the meal. Judith was a stickler for cleanliness. Her people were all that way. Washing morning and night no matter the weather, and she expected as much from everyone else, too.

"Your brothers brought more silver in today. I'll be

working on that for a few days I suppose." Thomas sat down heavily in the chair he had made himself. "They surely do bring in a lot of it. They must have a fine place to get it."

Judith ladled stew filled with rabbit and her fresh garden vegetables into his bowl. "They only take what they need. Fall will be here soon and they must go trade for goods to help the village through the cold months." She ladled soup into her own bowl and sat down. "They have offered to let you get some, too."

"I know, but I just have something against the very idea of letting someone lead me around blindfolded." Thomas broke a biscuit and dunked it in the stew broth. "It is kinda insulting that they don't trust me more than that."

Judith kept her eyes on her bowl. "They say the same of you not trusting them if they blindfolded you."

Thomas allowed the topic to drop, but it was not far from his mind. Wherever that silver was, he was determined to get some of it for himself.

As the months went by, his wife's people brought silver in to be worked into jewelry. Thomas tried to get hints about where this silver might be, but the Indian men were cagey and could not be tricked. He even tried following them a few times, but they only went back to the village and it seemed fruitless.

Finally Thomas realized that he had no choice but to accept the invitation, so he sent word that he'd like to accept his wife's family's terms about going for the silver.

On the appointed morning at least twenty men showed up at the smithy. They explained to him that he would be blindfolded the entire time and that they would not tolerate it if he tried to trick them.

Croyle had known the Indian people for many years and he accepted their terms quietly. He allowed himself to be blindfolded and subjected himself to being led around through the woods. The Indians were careful not to hurt him, but still he stumbled many times. Each time Croyle fell, he tried to feel something familiar. His fingers sought items that he might recognize again but there seemed nothing to help him. He must somehow remember the route they were taking but it seemed very circular and difficult.

After walking for nearly two hours, Croyle was led into a cave. Here the blindfold was pulled off and he saw by the light of pine knot torches a vast hole dug in the middle of the floor. Tumbled among the rocks were strains of silver such as Croyle had only dreamed about. Croyle dug and worked as he sorted and chipped away at the rock. He picked up a pile of silver nuggets and put them in his bag. While he worked, some of the Indians did the same, but others seemed to be standing guard.

Despite his best efforts, Croyle could find nothing that he recognized to help him figure out where he was. He desperately wished to note the location of the silver cave but he had no landmarks to go by. He allowed the blindfold to go around his head once more, but he felt a terrible desperation. Perhaps this was his one and only chance to figure out this mystery.

Croyle hit upon an idea as he began the long walk back to his home. Each time he stumbled he'd break a couple tree branches. He'd only break twigs that were easy to snap and quiet, but it would be enough so that he could trace his route back to the mine.

By the time Croyle and his party returned to his cabin and the blindfold was removed, the original party had dwindled down to only a handful of men. Croyle stashed his silver in his shop and thanked the Indians for their generous gift.

However, as soon as they were gone Croyle began tracing his path backward toward the mine. Very shortly he lost his trail and he knew that they could not have passed this way. The terrain was too rugged for him and he had not struggled so when he was going to the mine or coming back. Croyle found tree after tree with snapped branches. At last it dawned on him that there were many times the amount of branches he had actually snapped.

With a sinking feeling in his stomach, Croyle realized why the party of Indians had become so small at the end. They had grown wise to his trick and had decided to play sport with him. Several of the Indian men had begun breaking branches at random and those where what he was seeing. He had lost his chance to find the mine!

Croyle never did find that mine, but he often told his story of once seeing it. When the Snake Indians were driven from Bedford County, they took the secret of the mine with them. However, if you are wandering the woods and hills behind Hospital Hill in Bedford County and you chance upon a cave, well you could be the first person in over two hundred years to see the Lost Silver Mine of Snake Spring Township.

TARNISHED GOLD
(Blair County)

Visions of rich gold strikes have driven many people westward, but in Central Pennsylvania there was a man named Sam Kinney who in the early years of the Twentieth Century came to believe that a vast gold mine rested atop Tussey Mountain near his home. Local stories have long speculated that Sam Kinney became convinced of the gold mine due to nightly dreams in which he was shown where to dig. This story however, can no be confirmed and is probably as valid as the many other stories including one which intimated that he used "occult" means such as gold dowsing to locate where he should dig his mine. It has even been said that he was looking for a lost cow when he stumbled upon the gold.

At any rate, Sam Kinney decided that the mine should be located near the old wagon road that passed through Henrietta and onward to the town of Saxton in Huntingdon County. Along this road many a traveler had once trod on a westward trek when this area was rough frontier land in the early part of the 1700's. Kinney began by digging a couple shafts downward into the mountain.

Soon word of Kinney's Folly reached town. At first there was a lot of laughter and general fun poking at poor Sam Kinney. Everyone knew that there was no gold in Pennsylvania, except in the northernmost part of the state. However, soon good sense fell prey to gold fever. The little town of Martinsburg became a hotbed of gold fever speculation. Perhaps Sam Kinney was onto something and others did not want to miss out on a chance to get rich.

Things grew even more fevered when word reached the little villages and towns on both sides of Tussey Mountain that "Sam Kinney has found gold!"

Even the most skeptical critics of Sam Kinney's gold mine were no longer able to shake their heads and demand proof. Sam Kinney had come off the mountain with gold ore. Here was the proof they had long demanded. In a local newspaper it was described like this, "Marked with shining specks of yellow that looked like gold..."

Sam wasted no time in organizing the gold mine. He would need money to dig it out. He created a company complete with stock certificates, and he hired salesmen to go throughout the valley selling the stock. Some of the gold stock certificates still exist as proof of the mine.

Sam had his gold ore assayed and it was found to contain not gold ore but copper ore instead. Copper was good, too. Copper could make you rich and his stock certificates were still good. The metallurgist's report indicated that there was a heavy density of copper. Sam Kinney was still sitting pretty.

News of the metallurgist's report reached the ears of several large mining companies. The companies contacted Sam Kinney and wanted to send out their own metallurgists. Here is where the story gets difficult. According to the official version, the Cambria Iron Company sent out a metallurgist who did not confirm the findings of the other metallurgist. In fact, this man insisted that the mine was worthless and always had been.

With such news it was no surprise that rumors flew. One camp stated that Sam Kinney and his friends had salted the mine with gold in the first place to make a fortune off of the worthless gold certificates. A plausible idea except for the fact that no one--Sam Kinney included--ever made a fortune from the mine or the certificates.

The other camp insisted that the Metallurgist from the Cambria Iron Company had falsified the tests. This man was hoping to purchase the mine for himself they said. But the man didn't want the mine, and as no one gained from this theory it was soon dropped. The fact of the matter was that no one really knew what the truth was.

In the 1930's, a group of local men including a fellow named Jacob Benner, had another try at mining atop Tussey's Mountain. They cleared brush away from the abandoned mine and set it up. Despite high hopes and desperately hard work, no one found even an ounce of gold.

Today it would be almost impossible to locate the old Saxton Gold Mine, but up on that mountain there is a mine as tribute to one man's big dreams--whatever they may have been. As for old Sam Kinney, he and his gold mine were to become the laughing stock of the area for some years. If he set out to bilk his neighbors and steal their money, he had no luck with that either. If he was a dreamer who had a big dream then you can't help admiring the man.

This notation was taken from an issue of the *Morrison's Cove Herald*: *"When it eventually became known that the mine had been salted with iron melted with shavings of pennies and discarded odds and ends of copper, the stories retailed at the blacksmith shop during leisurely evenings were not nearly as robust and well worth hearing, as if the gold had been actually discovered.*

"No question about it, the Kinney gold mine hoax was the biggest practical joke that ever has been sprung in the Cove."

But for Sam Kinney and the men who invested in the mine, it wasn't much of a joke. Is there any truth to this tale? I'll leave this story with you to decide.

THE BETRAYAL OF BLACKBEARD'S TRUST

(Bucks County)

It must be made clear that though this story is about a Captain Blackbeard, it is not about Edward Teach, the famous Captain Blackbeard. This other captain, though, had an adventure worthy of his famous counterpart and was betrayed by a friend.

Captain Blackbeard stood upon the deck of his ship and watched as the last of the treasure of Spanish silver was lifted into his hold by his men. The hot sun of the Bahamas beat down upon his head, but Blackbeard was not interested in the weather. His mind turned with possibilities. He needed to get his trove back to London, but on the way he would have to be very careful. There was no way he could work the old 1680 ship wreck and not let his men know that he was pulling up silver bars of great richness. Now he had to worry about loose tongues and drink, and greedy men. He would have to plot a very safe and steady course back to London and this would mean stopping in Canada for supplies for the journey over the Atlantic.

Captain Blackbeard began the treacherous journey, and all went well until he came to American waters. There he encountered a French privateer called the Karthaus. The captain of the Karthaus began to show an interest in the cargo aboard Blackbeard's ship. In order to lose the French privateer, Blackbeard was forced to pull into Baltimore harbor. However, the captain of the Karthaus was not easily deterred and he sat just off the American waters awaiting Captain Blackbeard's return.

Now Blackbeard faced a tough decision. He could go back into open waters and risk a confrontation with the Karthaus, a prospect he did not feel up to. Or he could make arrangements to load his treasure aboard a British war ship and send it over to England safely, however that option was taken from him by the outbreak of the War of 1812.

Blackbeard decided that the best option open to him was to move the silver overland. He studied the maps between Baltimore and Canada and thought that though the map did depict mountains, it could not be that difficult to traverse them. However, Blackbeard underestimated the mountains of Pennsylvania.

Blackbeard loaded his silver bars upon 6 wagons and Blackbeard started on his overland trek, but it was much more difficult than this seafaring man had anticipated. By the time he reached Renovo, a new threat also reached his ears. The War of 1812 was then raging and he began to fear that if the Americans realized what his wagons carried they might liberate it from him as bounty of war because he was a British citizen.

Now this new threat forced Blackbeard into a desperate act. He would find a place to bury the silver, and then return to recover it after the war was over and he no longer feared loosing his hoard as the war booty.

When Blackbeard reached the mountains near Emporium, he found a place that he felt was secure. There he buried the silver bars and waited. From Emporium Blackbeard sent a message to a trusted friend of old, Colonel Noah Parker. He convinced Parker, a wealthy man, to come to Emporium where he then poured out his story. As proof of the validity of the tale, Blackbeard showed Colonel Parker a bar of pure Spanish silver.

Colonel Parker was so impressed with his friend's story that he sought out the owner of the land where the silver now lay and purchased it himself. Then he vowed to Blackbeard that he would himself stay in Emporium and watch over the cache until Blackbeard could return.

However, wealth is a funny thing. If you have great wealth, you always want more. For some people the thought of great wealth can effect their minds, and that was what seemed to happen to Colonel Parker, Captain Blackbeard's great and trusted friend.

Colonel Parker literally built a castle on the land overlooking the site where the silver was buried. He guarded it tenaciously and allowed no one--Captain Blackbeard included upon his land to look for it.

Captain Blackbeard would try many times to retrieve his silver, but he died penniless and obviously never completed his journey to London as a rich man. Colonel Parker, too, seems to have never retrieved the silver. For him the knowledge that it was there and his own possession seemed to be enough to satisfy his greed. If he felt anything because of his betrayal of a friend and the fact that his betrayal ruined Blackbeard's life, he never allowed it to interfere with his dedication to protecting the silver.

Only two men knew the exact location of the silver and both men died without revealing it to anyone. The only clue left to us is that it was buried near the castle and in a spot where the castle overlooked it. Until this day, no one has found the silver that cost Captain Blackbeard so very much--including the indignity of a betraying friend.

THE COUNTERFEITER'S CACHE

(McKean County)

1910

The housewife smiled as she saw grubby old Cyrus Cole shuffling down the sidewalk with his buckets full of berries. It was late summer and Cyrus was in the middle of his berry picking season. Most of the folks in the little town of Eldred and in the towns beyond of Larabee, Port Allegany and Bullis Mills knew Cyrus. He was a fixture in those places. He came and went in his baggy bum's clothes and sold muskrats, rabbits and berries as the seasons permitted. Though he never seemed to have much money on him, apparently Cyrus made enough to keep body and soul together. Of course, it wouldn't take a man that much money when he lived in a shack he had constructed of cast-offs and old wood in the swamps of Pennsy Marsh, just north of Eldred.

Cyrus went upon his way from house to house as he measured out generous amounts of blackberries to his regular customers. At many of the stops Cyrus had to make change for the women and he inevitably bit each coin he was given to test it's authenticity. It was a matter of habit with Cyrus and many of his older customers knew the habit so well that they did not even smile any longer at Cyrus's cautious ways. It was funny, however, that Cyrus would think that anyone in the little towns he ranged through would pawn off bad money on him.

Well it was funny to everyone except for a farmer who was sitting outside of the general store. The fellow was new to town and he would have passed for a long-time farmer with his easy attitude, but his eyes did give him away. He watched intently as the old man with his stubbly whiskers sold his wares. This was a government man and he was very interested in poor old Cyrus Cole.

The Secret Service agent named Inspector Nye leaned forward slightly to get a better look at Cyrus Cole as the old fellow shambled along.

"You got a hankering for berries, Matt?" asked the shop keeper as he stepped outside and observed the farmer/secret service agent's intent gaze. "If you do, why don't you go pick some berries out on your farm? Plenty of them up on the ridge. Probably ole Cyrus picked his up there himself. No sense paying for your own berries."

Matt flipped a calculated look at the shop keeper. "Don't like berry picking. Might as well buy them from the old guy and give him a bit of change. Lord knows he looks like he needs it."

The shop keeper hooted at that one. "I ain't never seen such a man as that one, no matter the season that ole boy has some change in his pocket and I mean silver and sometimes gold pieces as well. I never thought there was that many muskrats in Pennsy Marsh, either. Some folks think he's an eccentric fellow that struck it rich in the oil fields round here. Wouldn't that beat all? Cyrus Cole selling berries for a living and being a rich man!" With a laugh the shop keeper turned and went into the store.

Pennsy Marsh thought the Secret Service agent. He would have to go for a walk through that area and check it out. Someone else had mentioned that the old man had a cabin or shack of sorts in the marsh.

The farmer flipped the chair forward so that it was on all four legs again and stood up. "Best get going," he muttered as he stepped down and followed the old man for a ways.

Cyrus continued along his route without the slightest glance backward. He was, however, aware that the farmer was following him. In fact, he was aware of every new face he saw in the area. He wondered if the farmer was looking to find out where the berries had come from. Cyrus Cole had no idea that this new farmer was a government agent or that someone had noticed his ability to always have money despite what he looked like. Someone had, in fact, written to the Secret Service to tell them that if they were interested in where the phony gold pieces and silver half-dollars were coming from that were flooding southern Canada, New York state and the upper part of

Pennsylvania they should look at an old man named Cyrus Cole. The letter went on to say that the writer believed that Cyrus was minting the fake money in his shanty in the swamps between New York and Eldred, Pennsylvania. The person said that old Cyrus Cole hid the dies for the coins in his window sills. Whoever had written that letter seemed to have a great knowledge of Cyrus Cole and his activities. Inspector Nye suspected that it was one of Cole's own gang who gave him up in a fit of revenge for some slight. The writer added that Cole was the head of a counterfeiting ring and that he was a crafty man.

The federal agent realized that there was truth to the letter. He had been watching Cole for a while and had concluded that the man could not account for his cash with the sale of berries, rabbits, and muskrats. It was time to wire the Secret Service and tell them that they needed to get a search warrant for the Cole shack.

As the letter said, Cyrus Cole was a crafty man, and he was also a cautious one. He had been minting fake coins and then exchanging them for real ones throughout the area for quite some time. He was careful to range over a large area disbursing his fake money. He had a ring of counterfeiters who ranged from state to state passing the phony money on, too. By the Secret Service's estimate Cole had amassed a fortune from his scheme and they were dedicated to stopping the counterfeiter.

With a search warrant in hand, the federal agents descended upon Cole's shanty in the swamps. They literally tore apart the old cabin and found coin molds secreted in a compartment hollowed out beneath a window sill. The agents were awed by the quality of the counterfeit coin molds. They were among the best that they had ever seen. If the old man had made them himself, he had quite a talent for counterfeiting. But they could not find any counterfeit coins or even any of the fortune of real coins that Cole must have amassed.

Cole was arrested and sent to a prison in Warren, PA while the agents struggled to secure the information to get their conviction. They knew that a fortune was somewhere out in the swamps that would prove their case but, despite massive efforts, they never found it.

The Secret Service was left to speculate that old Cyrus Cole had buried the counterfeit coins as well as the real silver and gold. They concentrated upon the high ground where the swampy waters did not reach, and they centered their search in the swamps near Eldred because that seemed to be where Cyrus Cole was most often seen.

Cole was tried before a Federal Judge in Erie but he was set free for lack of evidence. The Secret Service was unable to produce either the real or counterfeit gold and silver that was hidden in the swamps.

Cole eventually returned to his swamps but he always feared that the Federal agents were still watching him--and they most probably were. He feared to dig up his phony and real fortunes and died a poor old man. To this day there has been no word that any of Cyrus Cole's cache has been found. Somewhere in the swamps near Eldred there lays a fortune yet to be discovered--at least that is what the Secret Service believed.

THE CROSSING

(Bedford County)

Sitting in the curve at the foot of a hill just one mile from Breezewood, the old house does not really stand out. In fact, it looks much like many of the other old farmhouses in the area built of gray and brown field stone. However, the very ordinariness of the house belies a great history. This house is only seen today from the back on Rt. 30. You must stop your car and go down to the creek, cross it and climb the hill beyond to get a proper view of this historic old building. It was built to look upon the Blue Juniata, where traffic came up the river when it was built. Behind the house there were only mountains and Indian trails when it was built in 1818 upon the foundation of the older, first tavern.

By the time the stone structure was built, the land and the name Juniata Crossing had become well known to the history books. At this spot a crude cabin stood and a man ferried passengers across the Juniata River. Here in 1758, Col. Henry

Bouquet built the first bridge across the span for his troop of men who were engaged in the Forbes Expedition to Fort Duquesne. When Col. Bouquet chose this spot, there was already a crude tavern owned by a man named James Martin on the land. Martin's Tavern was truly an outpost of civilization in a large and hostile wilderness. Bouquet built a stockade and fort there. The fort was called Martin's Fort and the stockade was used to move provisions, protect the white inhabitants and offer shelter for the soldiers, wagon masters and others traveling the trail from Carlisle to Ray's Towne (Bedford). The fort had 4 storehouses, a barracks 200 feet long and was said to hold 700 soldiers at one time. The fort raised livestock for the Forbes Expedition so that they had meat to eat.

Col. Bouquet's bridge was a massive and marvelous feat, his bridge was of heavy chain and it survived until 1818 when a second, wooden covered bridge was built across the river by the Chambersburg and Bedford Turnpike company. This covered bridge was a part of the toll road that those immigrating westward could travel. To do otherwise would have been virtually impossible, and a mute testimony to the many weary feet that traveled it still remains upon the mountainside where wagons cut ruts into the rocks that can still be seen today.

The current inn was built upon the foundation of the Washington Tavern by Hugh Dennison. By 1835, the tavern was a toll station under the ownership of a Mr. McGraw.

Here the stories drift into legend and there are two different tales of possible treasure upon the grounds.

During the era of toll roads, there was many a robber who plied his wicked trade upon those roads. Most merely robbed their victims but the most vicious of the thieves actually murdered their prey. Any journey was long, difficult and dangerous and the thieves made it more so. This was the era of the gentleman bandit *Davey Lewis and we know that Lewis frequented the tavern and inn during Mr. McGraw's time. It was said that he was welcomed by McGraw and often spent the evening drinking with travelers whom he had earlier made his victims. However, Davey Lewis did not harm his victims other than to make their load lighter by relieving them of their gold and silver coin.

Stories have long circulated that Davey Lewis buried his robbery loot in the caves along the Juniata River near the inn, under the inn itself, or near the old fort just down the river from the inn.

There is, however, another story that makes even more sense. If Davey Lewis was so welcomed at the Juniata Crossings, it might have been because Mr. McCraw was a crony of his. There have long survived stories that Mr. McGraw would wait until travelers tried to enter the covered toll bridge at the far side, he'd step from behind a rock or tree with a cloth over his face and demand their money at gun point. The frightened travelers capitulated and counted themselves lucky to be allowed to pass across the bridge to the safety of the Juniata Crossings. McGraw would stash his loot somewhere near the bridge and hurry back across the water to meet the frightened travelers on the other side. He'd calm their fears, offer them the shelter of the Crossings and commiserate with them about the fact that someone must surely do something about the bandits that were preying upon travelers along the toll roads. On occasion, if he liked a family, McGraw might even offer them a small stake of their own money to help them as they headed to Fort Bedford.

McGraw supposedly hid the money from his robberies throughout the woods along the far side of the bridge. It is believed that to this day part of McGraw's money and some of Davey Lewis's loot are still hidden upon the grounds around the Juniata Crossings. It is amazing how the historical record of this particular spot has survived. There are drawings and plans of the fort and the remnants of the bridge that survive to this day. The pilings are still spread across the Juniata, and perhaps along them or further up toward Bloody Run (Everett) there is a treasure of ill-gotten loot awaiting discovery.

For more stories about Davey Lewis check out the story entitled Davey Lewis, Gentleman Bandit.

THE SECRET OF OLD FORT HORN

(Clinton County)

Independence from Great Britain was a treasure much sought after by our founding fathers and indeed they did find it. The United States Declaration of Independence would become not only one of America's most treasured documents, but one of the world's most treasured. It was proof that a dependent colony could successfully win their freedom from the mother nation. It was proof that freedom is one of our most valued treasures of all. Of course, the United States Declaration of Independence is well cared for by a staff of curators and document specialists, but did you know that there is another American Declaration of Independence that has never been found? This document's story is the stuff of legends, except that this story is absolutely true.

Fort Horn at Pine Creek was built in 1773 for the defense of the local population from Indian attacks. The area was Indian territory by treaty, but that did not stop whites from settling the territory. The English who settled there set up an independent government known as the "Fair Play" government. This government allowed for a three-man panel of commissioners to rule upon land and legal disputes. This system was known as the "Fair Play System. "Because the men were illegally living on Indian lands, they answered neither to the British government nor to the fledgling American government that was just beginning to shape itself. Men from this area were in contact with the delegates of the Second Continental Congress in Philadelphia who were drafting the Declaration of Independence.

On July 4 of 1776, a Declaration of Independence was written and signed locally declaring the independence of the American squatters from British rule. This document was given various names, it was the "Pine Creek Declaration of Independence," the "Tiadaghton Document" or as the "Fair Play Document." All three names were accurate descriptions, but one name actually could offer clues to the whereabouts of the document. The Tiadaghton Document name refers to where the document was signed.

The squatters built two forts in the area. One was Fort Horn built at the mouth of the west branch of the Susquehanna. This area was known as a plain or barrens area because it had been cleared of trees long before by natives and was said to be the site of large Indian towns long before. The whites called the creek Pine Creek, but the Indians called it Tiadaghton Creek. There was a lone elm tree in that area and this tree became a reference point for both nations. It is said that it was under this elm tree that the actual document declaring independence from England was signed.

The document was copied and the original placed in a watertight pouch that was then placed in an iron box. The box was buried for safe keeping. The document appears to have been written within hours of the United States Declaration of Independence, and those who had read both documents stated that they bore an uncanny resemblance in content.

Before the original document was sealed up, two copies were made which were dispatched with two riders, Michael Quigley Jr. and Patrick Gilfillen, who were to deliver them to the Second Continental Congress. Both men were attacked by Indians and subsequently delayed. The men did not arrive at Philadelphia until July 10. Then they found out about the American Declaration of Independence and read it. They had both lost their copies of the Pine Creek document during the Indian attacks, but they vouched for the amazing resemblance between the two documents. They took word back to the Fair Play squatters, and the Pine Creek document seems to have been left alone after that. There are stories that other important documents were also in the packet that had been buried that day.

However, the Pine Creek Declaration of Independence was doomed to never be seen. The Indian Wars heated up and people began to flee for their lives. The Iroquois Confederacy joined forces with the British to attack the settlements in the Fort Horn and Pine Creek area. The entire area was virtually razed by fire. Most of the homes and the fort were burned down.

It was not until 1779 that General Sullivan pushed back the Iroquois Confederacy and restored peace to the Pine Creek area. By then the topography of Fort Horn was vastly changed. The structures were gone and it was impossible to locate the exact spot where the iron box had been buried.

Throughout the early years of peace, people did attempt to locate the Pine Creek Declaration of Independence but they were not successful. Today the value of this document is beyond imaging. It would literally be priceless. Museums, historical institutions and private collectors would vie for such a rare treasure.

However, this story is not without its detractors. There are historians who claim that the entire event never happened. In fact, many scoffed at the oral traditions that kept the story alive. With due respect to their opinions, many other historians do believe that there is truth in this old tale. We do know that many parts of the story are true. Many of the people named in the story did live in the area and were part of the Fair Trade System. Fort Horn and the Tiadaghton elm did exist. In fact, the elm was not cut down until the 1970's. Old maps do exist showing that Tiagdaghton Creek or Pine Creek did and does exist. It would not be an easy matter to figure out the location of the documents and there is a possibility that they would not be salvageable today. One can only wonder what over two hundred years in the ground has done to the document. The United States Declaration of Independence is well kept, but this document was sealed up in the ground. How long would it take the iron chest to rust or be corrupted by water? Did the water tight seal hold the packet or did it break down? There is a very good chance that the document is destroyed or damaged. But if it is intact, and if it were to be found, it would be a treasure hunter's wildest dream come true. The search for such a specimen would require a great deal of painstaking research, but to hold this bit of history would be amazing and the finder might never have to work again. Beyond that, it would be a national treasure that we could all admire-- and the story is the stuff that movies are made of.

DABOLE'S GOLD
(Clearfield County)

Dabole Hare stood up from his work and looked around. It was the summer of 1850 and he was reminiscing as he inspected his farmlands. Before him were the crops that he had planted with his own hands. He was a proud man who had done well for himself. When he and his wife had come to settle on their farm in Halfway Hollow near Roulette in 1830, they had been much younger. Through the years, they had built a wonderful life. Dabole had been a savvy businessman as well as a gifted farmer. The combination had made him quite wealthy. Dabole had a few steadfast rules in life and one of them was that he'd only accept gold coin in trade for work or products. He wasn't too sure of paper money. It was easy to counterfeit it or steal it. Worse yet, paper money could be destroyed easily. Whereas gold, would withstand a great deal more before it was destroyed and even if it was melted down, gold held its value.

Another of Dabole's rules was that he didn't trust anyone, including banks, with his gold. Dabole was an independent sort who remembered the days of counterfeiters. He read the newspaper articles about how folks were devastated by a bank robbery. Dabole would trust his own wits to protect his fortunes, and to that end, he hid his gold himself.

Yet another of Dabole's rules was that one never put all their eggs in one basket. So Dabole hid his gold coins in several places around the farm. At any given time, Dabole could pick up his trusty shovel and dig up whatever gold he needed. As a matter of fact, Dabole had divided it up so well that he couldn't rightly remember just where all he had buried his treasure. His family knew about his habit of burying the family gold, but Dabole was not willing to tell his secrets to anyone. Even his own wife had no idea what they had or where it could be found.

For months, Dabole tried to recover his various treasures but he knew that he was missing some. He would dig them up, and then rebury them throughout the farm. Some were around the barns where only he would go. Others were located at various secluded spots around the property.

Dabole's family occasionally questioned him about the whereabouts of his gold. "You're not going to live forever," his daughter pointed out one night. "Papa you need to tell us where it is so that we can locate it if we ever need to."

Dabole knew that his girl was right, but the idea of others knowing about his gold was too much for him. One day, he promised himself, he'd tell them, but only when he got so old that he couldn't get around anymore. Even when Dabole's wife passed away he kept his secret. He'd take his daughter into his confidence one day, he promised himself, but not yet. He even thought about confiding the truth to his son-in-law, George Lehman, whom he knew to be a good and just man, but still the idea of telling about his gold just didn't sit easy with Dabole and so he put it off.

After his wife's death, his daughter insisted that he visit her house more often. One evening Dabole was expected for dinner but he did not arrive. George Lehman set out to see what had happened to his father-in-law. The path between the two houses was fairly easy going, except perhaps at the Allegheny River. George walked back the path hoping to meet the old man, but he did not see him anywhere. He had to go home to his very worried wife and tell her that her father was not home and that he was not on the path either. The Lehman's called a search and with the help of neighbors found Dabole's body in the river. He had slipped, fallen and drowned.

After the first wave of grief subsided and Dabole was decently buried, the Lehman family had to figure out what to do with the Hare farm. George thought about selling it but his wife told him about the old man's caches of gold coins. It seemed a relatively easy task to find the gold at first but after numerous searches they had uncovered nothing. Eventually the family took others into their confidence and offered a portion of the gold to anyone who helped them find it. Still not a single coin was ever recovered. Dabole's daughter knew that her father had hidden caches of gold throughout the property but it was never located. Eventually the property was sold and the farm divided up. If any of the Dabole Hare farm still is accessible, then the gold is still out there somewhere waiting for someone to find it. Perhaps, though, Dabole is also out there keeping watch over his fortune. German tradition has it that a man can not rest if he buries secreted gold and does not dispose of it by the time of his death. The Pennsylvania German folklore is rife with tales of ghosts haunting until they can find someone to listen to them as they divulge the location of hidden gold. There are also tales of ghostly fires that mark the spot where such gold can be found. Perhaps by now Dabole is ready to tell the secret and part with his hidden gold.

THE CURSED TREASURE OF HUCKLEBERRY HILL
(Montgomery County)

Through the years I have never ceased to be amazed at how many times perception and truth are separated. There has got to be no better case of this than the story of William Penn. Penn has long been painted as this great humanitarian who stood for freedom and justice and who treated all people with dignity and respect. Yet historical data proves that this is not exactly the case. Being a Quaker he did speak, write and generally espouse such a philosophy of equality, but he was also a nobleman of great wealth and in real life he and his family often did not live up to what they claimed to believe. There are many such incidents that could be brought forth to illustrate this truth. For example, William Penn claimed to be against slavery, yet he owned many slaves himself. He spoke out to insist that other people free their slaves, but his own slaves were never freed until after William Penn's death. Penn also claimed to treat the natives of this land with dignity and respect, however, many a native would have a different story to tell.

Among those disgruntled with William Penn because he "bought" land from them was Chief Wessapoak of what is now Montgomery County. Chief Wessapoak did not know that he was selling his land until he and his people were driven out in 1683 by white colonists who claimed that the Chief had sold it to William Penn, and that they had bought it from Penn. Wessapoak was not a naive man, and he knew that there were valuable minerals on the ground in dispute. Of course, this is probably why Penn decided to "purchase" this ground. When Wessapoak lay upon his deathbed, he still felt the burning hatred for those who had driven him from his home. He uttered a curse upon the ground that no white man would ever profit if he tried to procure riches upon that ground.

How the whites came to know of this dying curse I do not know, however, it was apparent that soon thereafter, the land became known as cursed, haunted, or under a spell.

Chief Wessapoak knew the white man well and soon the interlopers began looking for wealth upon the cursed land. Stories surfaced that there was silver upon Huckleberry Hill, and this tale was bolstered by old legends that came down to the white men. People began to whisper about a secret silver mine the Indians had hidden before they left the area.

The story of the silver mine actually dates back to at least 1697. Captain Hans Moen sailed the *Pennepack Dreek* into what is now Montgomery County looking for a silver mine that he heard about from the native people down stream upon the Pennepack. Apparently, Captain Moen did not find the treasure because others soon followed him. Many listened to the old tales of the natives that indicated that the silver mine was on what they called Huckleberry Hill.

One man became obsessed with the idea of finding that lost silver mine; he was a German named Derrick Kroons. Kroons was the son of a farmer who had originally settled that area. His father had come from the Palatine to settle in the New World and Derrick had grown up hearing of the lost silver mine of Huckleberry Hill. As a young man, he lived near the hill in a stone house with his wife and children. His property was quite nice by standards of the day, with clapboard fences, a log barn and beehives, it was a nice little farm. However, Kroons was not satisfied with his life. Kroons had great dreams and at the center of his dreams was the tale of the lost silver mine.

Kroons was known by his friends and neighbors to wax poetic about the mine, and one December night, while a group of friends and neighbors were gathered around Kroons kitchen table, the talk once again shifted to old stories of the lost mine.

One of the men in the group, an Irishman, voiced his

belief that there had to be silver threaded through those hills. He told stories of other places in the New World where great reserves of silver had been discovered already. As the Irishman made his case for the silver mine, Derrick Kroons felt as if he alone was listening to this conversation. What the Irishman said made sense.

Another fellow insisted that a local dowser, Anthony Larry, had found a spot on Huckleberry Hill where a well should be dug. "Aye, that silver mine is there and that's not a doubt. Anthony Larry has found it with his rods. I know this for a fact and can prove it to ye. Did you notice the quality of the buckles upon his shoes? They are of the finest silver and he dug it up himself upon Huckleberry Hill. But, Anthony, the devil don't want to be sharing the wealth. If we could locate that mine for ourselves, we'd not a one of us ever have to toil in the soil again." The farmer looked around the table at his fellows. "We could hold our heads high and there'd not be a man of land in the country who could look down upon us then."

When the group finally said good night, Derrick Kroons could not sleep. That night he vowed that he would find that silver mine and that nothing in this world would stop him. Derrick was as good as the vow he made to himself.

The next morning Derrick began to search the land looking for where this well that Larry Anthony had dug was located. He searched from December until March before he located what he believed to be the spot where Anthony had dug the virgin ore for his shoe buckles.

The spot that Kroons fixed upon was in a ravine not more than half a mile from his own home. He kept his quest silent and made excuses to his family for he prolonged disappearances. He would be gone for long days before returning dirty, exhausted and silent. When he returned he'd be carrying a shovel, but he refused to tell even his own wife what secret task he was bent upon.

Stories began to surface about Kroons strange disappearances and his odd behavior. People began to speculate upon why he was disappearing and what he could possibly be up to. Not a soul asked him any questions though, for the German grew furious when the subject was broached.

After a particularly long absence, Kroons' wife grew quite worried. She was afraid of what could have happened to her husband and finally she sought out the hired man, Fritz, to ask him to help. She told Fritz that she feared some hard times had befallen her husband and she sent him to ask the neighbors if they could mount a search party. Just before dawn the following morning, Fritz and a group of neighbor men took to the woods. Throughout the long spring day the men stomped through the woods, over hills and down ravines. As darkness threatened, Fritz turned back to the farm but on the way he came past the little ravine and something made him decide to veer off into it. Darkness had fallen and a cold March wind had sprung up. The sound of tree branches clicking against each other was the only sound in the darkness. As Fritz walked cautiously through the darkness, something suddenly struck him in the face. Reacting to the feel of cloth, he raised his hands and found that he had grabbed hold of a man's coat. In the last of the twilight, he quickly recognized that the coat belonged to Kroons.

Fritz began to look around more carefully and found that he had stumbled into a crude clearing where a deep hole had been dug in the earth. A gasp of terror caught in Fritz's throat for a pale hand was protruding from the dirt and was grasping to a tree root. A step closer let him see the near-dead face of Derrick Kroons just barely peeking through the earth. Kroons had been buried alive in the hole.

In desperation Fritz began to dig to free his boss. He dragged and carried Kroons back to the farm where Kroons' wife took over. The farmer was bruised and stiff, starved and thirsty, but his good wife attended him until he was well.

In the meantime the story of the hole in the ravine, of Derrick Kroons being buried alive, and of the silver mine made the rounds. Curious neighbors came to inspect the site but found no silver, so they filled in the hole.

Kroons was said to have lost his ability to speak because of his harrowing experience and he never again went into that cursed ravine. What had happened and how he came to find himself in that predicament were questions never to be answered. It was said that stories of the silver mine in that ravine continued on for many years until after Derrick Kroons family finally sold the farm in the late 1800s. The auctioneer that day bellowed to those gathered to bid, "Come on folks, it's sure there is gold upon this land!" as a way to raise the bidding. Gold or silver, it didn't really matter because old Wessapoak's curse would prohibit white men from profiting from that land.

Kroons experience seemed to end any real desire to find the lost silver mine. Still, just below the surface of the minds of those who have long lived in the area, there is still that distant hope that one day they might be digging and be the one to find the lost silver mine of Huckleberry Hill. However, there must be mixed feelings about such a find for it is possible that Chief Wessapoak's curse will still ring true through all those centuries if the mine is ever unearthed.

THE MURDER OF SHARKEY
(Somerset County)

This story was written before the Windber Hotel was purchased by the current owner. This gentleman has worked hard to redo the grand old hotel and he has certainly succeeded. Bit by bit he is reclaiming this grand old dame of a structure and it is certainly worth a visit today. The story below is told as it was told to me that day years ago when I first visited the Windber Hotel and by the old man who once owned it.

I never seem to know when I'm going to find a good story. This story of lost treasure just fell into my lap one day when I was visiting with some friends. It was a day when I had decided to play hooky and I wasn't going to work at all, but when my friend dropped a sheet of paper in my lap and asked me to read it, well I just couldn't resist.

The paper was a printout from a website and it was about a group that had recently gone through the Windber Hotel. It was an interesting little story, but they made little mention of the fact that there was a lost cache of money involved. However, my friend suggested that the hotel was nearby and that we should go check it out.

I soon found myself in the back of his car on my way to the Windber Hotel. I have to admit that at first sight I was disappointed. The hotel was not grand by any standard. It clearly once was, but when I first saw it, the building looked aged and the facade was cracking like make-up on an old lady. I didn't really know what to expect when I stepped through the door. What I found myself in was a bar. It was an average bar in many ways. It certainly didn't promise much by way of a haunting, but I walked up to the bartender, Jeff, and offered my hand as I explained who I was. The grin on his handsome young face told me that he was receptive to ghost hunters; but that didn't mean that the owner would be.

Jeff summoned the then owner, Lee, and he stuck out a large hand and offered a big grin. "Come on in", he said with a smile. He invited us to tour the building and even relieved Jeff of his bar duties to accompany us and tell us the many tales of the Windber Hotel.

I'll chronicle the ghost stories in another place (and believe me there are many ghost stories about this building), but Jeff caught my attention when he showed us where a set of stairs used to be and where a trap door to the basement had been covered up. He also introduced me to a character from Windber's coal mining history named Sharkey.

Sharkey bought the Leister Hotel in 1902 and ran it for approximately ten years. He had bright wallpaper with big orange flowers on it placed on the walls of the bar and it became Sharkey's Orange Lounge. It was a spot where the more genteel of Windber's society could congregate upon an evening. Below their feet, however, was another bar that was much seedier. It was literally a basement room that had been crudely turned into a bar for the coal miners. Here men covered with coal dust could slake their thirst before returning home bone weary and perhaps a little sicker from their long confinement under the earth. Sharkey didn't miss a trick, and though the upstairs clientele paid well, he made a great deal of money from the dirty coal miners, too.

Apparently Sharkey didn't trust banks so he had a safe secreted in the basement labyrinth of rooms where he could keep control of his own money. Each night he'd go down the basement stairs with the day's receipts and disappear for a bit. When he re-emerged, he had deposited the money in that secret place.

One evening Sharkey followed his normal routine and walked down the stairs. He was directly under the trap door when suddenly he crumpled. A single shotgun blast had peppered his back and Sharkey lay bleeding to death. Whoever the murderer was, he quickly gathered the scattered money and disappeared. Sharkey died in that spot in the cold, damp basement and legend has it that he still haunts that area protecting his money from thieves.

Such a fine tale assuredly caught my interest, and this tale was very fine for it actually had a basis in historical fact. There had been a man named Sharkey and he had owned the hotel, he had been shot in the back carrying down the day's receipts, and he had kept his money somewhere in the basement.

I could see exactly what must have happened, and yet there was one point in the story that I didn't quite feel comfortable with. How could there be a secret safe hidden within the stone walls of this dank, old basement, and how could such a safe have eluded the more than curious eyes of subsequent owners?

Still, that night my focus was on ghosts so I dropped the topic and went back to collecting ghostly tales. I wouldn't again think of those questions until about a month later when we finally came to spend a night in the haunted Windber Hotel.

During the evening our focus was primarily upon ghosts, but my friend and I were both apparently keeping the notion of treasure in our minds, too. We walked the basement time after time getting the "feel" of the place. We found ourselves tramping the cold, cement hallways past mounds of debris from past owners that Lee was still trying to weed through. We found nothing to speak of, but there was just something about one area in the main hallway of the basement that kept drawing me back. It just seemed to keep calling to me. Here I was flanked by stone walls on both sides. I looked up and saw the trap door above my head. Those stone walls, I realized, must have once been splattered with Sharkey's blood. As I stood there thinking of poor Sharkey and his terrible end, I suddenly seemed to be struck by a great conviction. Starkey was a frugal and savvy man. He had these lovely stone walls all through the basement so why would he waste money on a wall safe when he literally had hundreds of other spots to hide the money. I just felt with every fiber of my being that Sharkey had hid his money in a box behind those stones somewhere.

I began to touch the stones, to gently prod at them, but none gave way. It was a good idea I thought at last, but either I'm wrong or else I'm just not looking in the right spot. I began to move on, and in the semi-darkness I had to glance down to see where I was stepping. A glint caught my eye. Money...! I bent over and picked it up. The nickel turned out to have been minted in the 1950s, but then I caught sight of another coin, a penny, 1967 it read, and my eyes moved on to another coin. Soon I had gathered about seven coins from the dirt below the wall where I had been looking. My friend snapped a photo of me collecting the money. I don't know why, but I felt immensely gratified and enchanted by that old money. It was almost as if Sharkey was teasing me by saying, "You're on the right track, girl, but not quite good enough. My money is still safely here." I went on, but found myself repeatedly returning to that area. Would I be the one to whom Sharkey would reveal his secret?

Late in the evening, I quietly slipped away from my friends and made my way back to the basement. I went directly to where Sharkey had died. He had been coming down to hide the day's receipts. He didn't have much time and it had to be easily accessible. Where did he hide his money?

Suddenly I heard footsteps and my friend came into view. He had noticed that I had wandered off by myself. He scolded me but I quickly explained why I was there. I could see the light gleam in his eyes as I spoke. He was enchanted with the treasure tale, too. We talked and my friend agreed that probably Sharkey did hide his moneybox behind the stones of the walls. It was such a convenient place.

My friend and I lingered in the basement a while longer. I felt drawn to one of the walls behind us and made a beeline for a certain stone about two-thirds of the way up the wall. I pulled it gently and it gave in my hand. Behind it was a small pile of dust and debris that I gently scooped out. Beyond that there was a cavity that should not have been in the wall. It was scooped out and was big enough to hide a small box or a bag. Somehow I felt that Sharkey was revealing part of his secret to us.

Did he hide the money there and was it taken by the murderer? I guess no one will ever know unless Sharkey decides to tell us. Of course, careful Sharkey probably didn't hide all of his money in one place. So either the treasure was taken by the murderer or else it's still there behind one or more walls in that basement and Sharkey was just having a good time with us that night. Either way, I don't really care. I broke a personal rule that night and took something from the site home with me. I took those few coins and keep them as a reminder of my first treasure hunt...

Those coins are still with me and I hope to have them framed. They are certainly too new to have come from Sharkey's stash, but I think he put them there to tease me. They gave me a brief thrill, and now I understand better why people hunt treasure. For me they will always remain a gift from a ghost and a symbol of one of my personal favorite treasure tales.

THE RAIDER'S TREASURE
(Adams County)

Gettysburg will forever be associated with that epoch battle that took place there in July of 1863. In many respects the battle of Gettysburg was not unique. In countless other places the Union forces had clashed with the Confederates who were fighting for their own right to create a separate union. In countless other spots the dead and wounded had gone by virtually unnoticed except by those in the area and the loved ones who had lost so much on those fields of battle. But in the annals of American history, Gettysburg was also a very unique place. It was a spot where the great generals of both sides fought the best and most desperate battle. Perhaps they both knew that the outcome of this single battle would mark the tides of the war. It was an unplanned battle in many respects. Lee never meant to engage such large forces in and around that little Pennsylvania village.

Even the men who would participate never realized that they were facing the most tremendous battle of their lives. In fact, most of the Confederate forces were not thinking of epoch battles at all, they were thinking of food, shoes, clothes and other valuables which could buy such necessities. The Confederate forces were in desperate shape. Some of them were not merely ragged, but they were literally barefoot and starving. In McConnellsburg, Fulton County, the first Confederate casualties of the Pennsylvania Campaign were shot. The Confederate men were raiding farms and stealing whatever food, clothing or valuables they could find

Colonel E.V. White's mission was to destroy the railroad lines in Harrisburg and thus interrupt the supply lines. It was Colonel White's Confederate forces who supposedly came upon a peddler who had a wagon loaded with valuables. The wagon was one of what were known as sutler's wagons. These were merchants peddling goods to the Union Army. However, with the Confederates in the north and the Union Army arriving from the south, the sutlers found themselves in the middle and were not well liked by the Confederates for many reasons.

The peddlers were stopped by the forces and questioned as to the movements of the Union Army. The wagons were also searched and any money confiscated. In the course of looking through the goods, an officer realized that one wagon was loaded with items stolen from various homes in Virginia. There were gold and silver picture frames with photos of loved ones still in them. There were silver dinnerware sets from various fine homes, but there was also an amazing amount of jewelry and gold stolen from the same plantation homes. The soldiers questioned the peddler and he confessed that he had taken the jewelry and wealth from various Virginia homes after they had been decimated by Union forces on the march south. Infuriated by this northerner's gall at stealing from Confederate families, the soldiers beat the peddler and left him for dead. The soldiers took charge of the wagon. They realized that this fortune could be sold for food and ammunition at a later date. The forces decided to bury the wagonload of valuable gold so that they could return later for it when they were sure they could gain safe passage back south. According to the soldiers who later told the story, they buried the fortune near where they had first discovered it-- on Old Hanover Road between Gettysburg and Hanover. They had only taken it a short distance toward Hanover Junction. The soldiers had every intention of coming back for the jewelry and gold in a few days, but the next day the battle of Gettysburg started. By July 3rd , the landscape had drastically changed and many of those who knew where the fortune was buried were either wounded or dead. The few remaining men were driven back south and never were able to return for the fortune left there. Some of them told family members about the treasure in hopes that one day they could retrieve it. Others told Union officers after they were captured about the buried loot in hopes of better treatment. No one was ever able to locate the buried cache again. It very well might still be buried somewhere between Hanover Junction and Gettysburg. There is not a record of it ever being discovered.

If the stolen bounty still exists, it would be worth several times more than the actual value of the gold in today's market. The story attached to the jewels and gold, and their age would lend greatly to their value.

THE SECRET OF TIONESTA

(Forest County)

Perhaps there is no other legend of a lost mine in the state of Pennsylvania that holds more interest than that of the lost silver mine at Tionesta. By the late 1600's, the local inhabitants of the state had come to realize that white men placed great value upon certain metals that came from the ground, and that those metals could help them get provisions that they needed. The native people had long used those metals for making ornaments, but they were quickly learning that silver and gold would get them supplies. Unfortunately, those same metals could also get them killed.

As the whites settled the land, they also taught the

natives about the value of another substance that was found where silver is present--lead. Lead was in its own way even more valuable to the average person than silver. Lead made bullets that could feed your family, or bullets that could protect them. But it also made bullets that could kill the natives, too.

There was a large Lenne Lanape village located across the river from the town of modern day Tionesta. In fact, Tionesta is an Indian word.

As more and more white men settled the area, the natives found that their way of life was forever changing. Hunting became secondary to trading for goods to sustain them. Trading furs could earn the natives a good living, but there were many white men out trapping to trade, too. It was not long before some of the best fur animals had disappeared from the area.

The natives had long been harvesting silver from a mine in Tionesta Valley which they used to make their jewelry. The early whites showed a great interest in the trinkets and the natives realized that this metal was a tradable good. The whites noticed that the natives near the village of Tionesta would go into the woods and return later with bags of silver ore.

Despite the many inducements offered them, the natives steadfastly refused to divulge the whereabouts of the silver and lead mine. They understood that if just one white man knew of the site, they would no longer own the mine that they had long used.

The story of the Tionesta silver mine would have remained just a legend except for several other stories that are connected to it.

A man by the name of Hill lived in the area of Tionesta during the 1700's. One day the man was hunting when a terrible storm sprang up. The man struggled to find shelter and stumbled upon an opening where he thought he might be able to shield himself from the pelting rain if he could just squeeze into it. The man was amazed to find himself squeezing through a small fissure into a cavern. By the light of his flint and the bit of daylight that leaked through the fissure he saw that the cave was littered with lumps of silver ore upon the ground. The walls were streaked with silver veins.

When the storm was over, Hill struggled back through the narrow opening and noted the spot in his mind. However, he was extremely excited by his find and he ran to tell his family about it. Hill estimated that he had found the cave about one mile north of where the Allegheny River passes the village of Tionesta. Unfortunately for Hill, he was never able to find the spot again. The native's silver mine was safe.

There are two other stories of whites seeing the mine. According to another story, two drunk white men stumbled into the cave opening and were awed by a pit in front of them that had been mined for silver. Chunks of raw silver lay strewn around them and they, too, hurried away to tell others of their great find. They thought that they were about to be rich men. However, like the luckless Hill, they could not find the mine again.

A local trader and trapper became a friend to the native villagers and he begged them to help their friend. The natives were by nature generous people and so they decided to share their wealth with their white friend. However, he had to agree to be blindfolded, bound and led to the mine. The man agreed because he was sure that if he could but see it once, he would be able to find it.

The white man was amazed to find himself in an impressive large cave that he had to crawl into with the help of his native guides. With the light of the pine stumps that the natives held, he saw a large pit with silver in it and strewn around it. The metal gleamed from veins in the walls. He was allowed to gather a small amount and place it in a bag. The man tried desperately to retain some sense of direction but the natives marched him through miles of trails before returning him home and the fellow was forced to be content with the gift from his friends instead of taking their entire mine as his own.

The stories lingered for many years until the 1970's, when *Treasure Magazine* looked into the tale and found that there just might be more to the legend than just old stories. Precious metals are unique and a good jeweler can actually look at gold or silver and tell where it came from. There has been antique silver from the early 1700's that cannot be pinned to any known mine. This silver has been traced to the Tionesta area. It is believed that it was mined from the Indian mine.

The story of the mine ended when the whites finally drove the natives away from their homelands. It is said that the natives took with them as much silver as they could easily carry to help their exodus, but that they also hid the mine entrance with rocks so that no white men would benefit from their mine. To this day no one has ever claimed to have found the silver mine of Tionesta--but still the stories persist. Perhaps in the wilds near the town of Tionesta a silver mine last mined by the Lenne Lanape is awaiting discovery.

REGRET

(Chester County)

The love of money is at the root of many a man's downfall. Could there be any argument that Judas Iscariot regretted selling out Christ for thirty pieces of silver? The money did him no good for he hung himself and let the money lay on the ground. How many times have people been sold out for money? Even in little ways, today, folks will sell out a friend for money. Though the man's name is no longer remembered, there is an old story dating from just after the American Revolution that offers proof that regret can destroy a life.

All those who knew the old man called him grumpy or rude. In truth, the old fellow was a bit of a hermit and he didn't care a fig for social graces. He had few friends and really didn't seem inclined to want to be sociable. The old man lived in his hut in the woods and kept to himself. However, the old man did have some neighbors who felt that it was their Christian duty to check up on the old fellow from time to time. In the wilderness, people had to watch out for one another.

One evening, a neighbor was passing by the crude hut when he noticed that no smoke escaped the chimney. The man wondered at that since it was quite cold outside. He decided to investigate and knocked upon the rough door to the little dwelling. For some time there was no sound and the man had turned to leave when he heard the coughing inside. He pushed open the door and called out, "Are you okay? Do you need help?" The room was cold as a tomb inside and the darkness beneath the thatched roof sent shadows scurrying about. The old man only coughed again in reply and made a low rattling sound in his chest.

"Be still," the neighbor called. "I'll build you a fire and fetch the doctor." The neighbor man quickly gathered some kindling from the woods and an arm load of thicker branches that he stepped on to break up. He took the wood and the kindling inside. He hurried back out and plucked handfuls of dried grass to act as tinder. He found an old flint atop the rude mantle and leaned over to strike it. In time he nursed a few sparks into a ruddy flame and fed the flames until the cracking promised that it would not die out. The fellow fetched some bigger wood and piled it on.

In the light from the fire, he saw the old fellow laying in a bed made of a pile of buffalo hides on the floor. The man was covered over by an old hide and seemed to shudder beneath the thickness of the skin. He was thin and the neighbor could find nothing for the old fellow to eat. He promised to return and hurried toward his own home. At the house, he sent his eldest son to fetch the neighbor woman who did some doctoring and asked his wife to pack him some stew in a crock to take back to the old fellow. The woman ladled up the stew and wrapped up some bread in a cloth. The neighbor man fetched some hard cider to give the man to drink and turned back to his chore. He was a kindly man and would not turn his back upon a neighbor in need, even a rude old man like the one in the primitive hut.

When the neighbor returned, the old man seemed surprised. The poor old thing was still shivering but not so badly now as the little fire had taken the worst edge from the chilled room. The neighbor fed the fire again and it crackled merrily. Then he set about heating the cider for the man and the crock of stew. The old fellow managed only a few sips of cider before falling back in his bed exhausted.

A knock upon the door brought the lady who did some doctoring. She brought along herbs that she set to brewing in a pan above the fire. She examined the old man and shook her head. She'd seen this before, pleurisy, and few in that condition could survive it. Still, through the night the neighbors toiled to tend the old fellow. The medicine woman's husband arrived and helped to keep the fire going through the night. By morning they could see that the old fellow was not improving.

It was a great surprise to all in attendance when the old man heaved a sigh and forced himself to sit up in bed. "I must tell this before I go," he wheezed. "Please listen and help me to make this right. During the (Revolutionary) War I pretended to fight for the Americans, but I was a spy. The British offered me gold coin for information, and so throughout my time in the military I sold them secret after secret. Men died because of me and my little cache of gold grew. I told myself that I was really being patriotic to my British government, and they promised that I'd be granted land and prestige for my treachery. But the Americans won, and I hid the gold for I could not explain it. I buried it outside not far from my hut. I've let it there ever since. Somehow spending it just seemed wrong. Now I must meet God and I am begging you to promise to dig up the gold and use it for some good. Perhaps if good comes of the money, God might forgive me for what I did and the lives I took. I have regretted what I did for a long time…" The old fellow fell exhausted back down in the bed. The neighbors did promise and tried to keep the promise, too. They attempted to find the gold many times, but the old man's directions were vague and so it was never found. The hut fell in and progress became the watchword of the new nation. The spirit of the old man, though, is said to still be waiting there near where he hid the gold for someone to dig it up and do good with it. Perhaps he is ready to reveal the secret to some likely soul. But remember, that gold has a way of changing a man, and a way of causing regrets if it's not properly used. The old man needs the gold to be turned to good use or else the treasure hunter might find that the old man will return to set things to rights.

JAKE SWANSON'S SECRET STASH

(Lackawanna County)

1928

Jake Swanson sat before the bank manager in his office in the north end of Scranton and glared at the man. "If that's the way of it," he roared at the arrogant banker, "I'll just take my money out of here!"

The bank manager winced at the loud voice and turned his head to breath without getting a whiff of old Jake's pungent odor. Jake made his living as a pig farmer and the stench of his livestock clung to his clothing and wafted in the direction of the bank manager.

"Mr. Swanson, please be reasonable. We simply can't acquiesce to your request. If we did,
then we'd have to do the same for every other customer who came in."

The rough old man looked at the bank manager through squinted eyes. "Seems to me, that I have more money in this here bank than most folks, so I should be entitled to some special treatment. 'Course, could be that you treat pig farmers differently than other folks cause you don't like our smell?"

The bank manger blanched. He hadn't been aware that his distaste for the old pig farmer had come through so clearly. He blanched for another reason, too. That old pig farmer was a very wealthy man. The bank manager knew that Jake had made a fortune raising his pigs for next to nothing. Jake had a route that he took every day throughout Scranton. He drove his rattle-trap truck around town gathering up the garbage from around the city. He stopped at nearly every restaurant, school and grocery store in town daily. He gathered the refuse into drums on the back of his old truck and hauled it away to his farm on Bell Mountain not far from the village Eynon. There the pigs were slopped with the waste and grew fat. Furthermore, Jake was a tight-fisted man who watched every penny he spent. The bank manager wondered if folks would have been so willing to give away things to the old fellow if they knew that he was far from the destitute pauper that he claimed to be. In fact, Jake was a very wealthy man. Now the bank manager attempted to smooth over the hurt feelings, but to no avail. Old Jake rubbed his whiskery face and shook his head.

"I've had about enough of your jaybobing around and I just wants out now. You go get me my money and I'll be leaving!"

The pleading and apologies of the Banker did nothing to sway the old man. He had had enough of the Banker's prissy ways.

In the end, the bank manager had to give the order to close out old Jake's account. But Jake went one step further. He didn't want a penny of his fortune in paper money. He wanted the whole thing to be given to him as silver dollars. Silver was more durable, more stable and safer to have around. The bank manager had not counted the cost too closely when he had refused old Jake's request and made him mad. Now the man saw that his foolishness was going to cost him. The teller who was attempting to fulfill Jake's request had come in to tell the manager that if he gave Jake all his money in silver dollars they might have to close the bank. A run on a bank could be the ruin of it. When folks thought that money was getting scarce, they all tried to get their money out at the same time further exaserbating the problem.

Old Jake went out and started his truck. He backed it around to the back of the bank and told the teller to fill up one of the washed out barrels he had brought to town to fill with pig slop. The barrel was turned up and the tellers began carrying out the heavy silver coins. By the time that they were done, half the fifty-five gallon barrel was full. Jake capped it like he did the other slop barrels and started off for his mountain home.

The bank manager nearly had to shut the bank down after Jake made his withdrawal. Times were already showing signs of stress and the major withdrawal found its way into general gossip. Soon other folks were coming in to take out their money, too. It took some fancy maneuvering on the part of the bank president for the institution to remain open.

Old Jake apparently returned to Bell Mountain with his loot in tact. No one ever saw the money again. What Jake did with the money became a mystery. Jake still lived like he was broke and never made mention of his fortune ever again.

Upon Jake's death a few years later, the bank manager notified the authorities that Jake had been in possession of a large fortune and inquiries were made at other banks. The money was never found. Jake had only three silver dollars on his person when he died. He did not appear to have done anything with the money. Folks speculated that Jake must have buried it on the farm. There were attempts made to find it, but not a one was successful. If that fifty-five gallon drum full of silver coins is buried on the farm on Bell Mountain, then it's still there waiting for someone lucky enough or enterprising enough to figure out where Jake Swanson hid his gold.

CARANTOUAN
(Bradford County)

In Bradford County there is a mountain once described as "a sugar loaf" mountain by early explorers. The mountain was called Carantouan on the oldest known maps from 1614 when Dutch map makers made a map of the area. Today the mountain is more commonly known as Spanish Hill. This name, too, is old and it hints at the mystery and possible treasure of Carantouan.

French explorer, Don de Rochefoucould-Lian-Court came to the area and wrote, "four or five miles to the north (of the junction of the Chemung and Susquehanna River) I saw a mountain ...upon which are to be found the remains of some entrenchments. The local inhabitants call them the Spanish Ramparts." Don de Rochefoucould-Lian-Court was referring to the vague remains of some sort of fortification that still remained on the mountain at that time. He began to talk among the locals and the natives and found an interesting tale. According to what he learned, there was a local legend that long ago, two groups of Spaniards (the natives called them metal hats) had come to the area to hide because they were being pursued. The Spaniards brought with them metal tools, swords and heavy chests of gold disks that they much valued. The Indians called the mountain "Hispan" after that. The Indians did not care for those men who hid their chests of gold disks in a cave upon the mountain. The Indians eventually attacked and killed the two groups of Spaniards, according to the legend.

Alpheus Harris was one of the surveyors who helped to survey out and affix the legal boundary lines between Pennsylvania and New York. While working in the Bradford County area he would write that he heard the legends of "Espana"or "Hispan" Mountain as some of the older natives persisted in calling it. He wrote of the legend of the gold, but he also added to the story. He insisted that local Indians would not approach the mountain known as Carantouan because they claimed that it was haunted by the ghosts of the metal hats who were protecting their chests of gold.

Through the years, many locals tried their hands at treasure hunting for the chests of gold. Perhaps the most famous person to search for the gold was none other than Joseph Smith, who would later be credited as founding the Mormon Church. In the 1820's, Smith spent time looking unsuccessfully for the treasure.

In the 1840's, there would be reason to revisit the legends. At that time, a Spanish medal dating from 1550 was found on the mountain. This spurred a furious search that unearthed a Spanish sword, a Spanish cross and the remnants of a Spanish-style boat. Suddenly, there was reason to believe the old stories told by the French which had been passed to them from the Iroquois who had gotten the stories from the now extinct Mound Builders. Could the Spanish relics found on the mountain mean that Carantouan was really the site where a vast fortune had once been hidden in a cave by Spaniards?

To this day, no one has ever located the cave where the gold is said to be hidden and where undoubtedly the Spaniards had taken refuge. At the very least, the cave would offer up countless artifacts and it could still contain a vast fortune in Spanish gold. It is certainly an unusual Pennsylvania treasure tale.

SILVER ARROWS
(Pike County)

When a fellow named Helm came to the area near Ice Mountain in the mid-1770's, he came for land, but he soon found that there might be great wealth in the mountains not far from Coudersport. Helm heard stories that the local Indians fought with silver tipped arrows, and that they were even shooting silver bullets. As amazing as it sounded, Helm thought it might be worth a look. He settled in the area. He sought out an acquaintance with the native people and eventually befriended a local chief. Through his proximity with the native people he came to understand that there was a cave up in the Shohola Glen area where the natives mined out silver ore. He waited and waited, but never did a single Indian give him a clue to where the fortune was hidden.

One day Helm managed to do something that impressed the chief of the tribe. Rumor has it that he saved the chief's little son from death. At any rate, the Chief decided that he needed to do something nice for Helm who had long been questing for the silver mine. He told Helm that he would personally take him to the mine, and then he did. What Helm hadn't factored in was that the chief would pay him back and still protect the silver.

Helm met the chief at Shohola Glen and allowed a hood to be placed over his head. The two men walked for some time and, despite Helm's best reckoning, he could not keep track of the trail. When Helm was allowed to lift the hood, he found himself in a cave of silver ore. The chief held a torch aloft and showed the man the vast fortune. Ore lay at Helm's feet and he gathered some into his pockets. Then he allowed the hood to be pulled back over his head. When he emerged, he was in Panther Brook Glen. Because of this, Helm always believed that there were two openings into the silver cave. One in Shohola Glen, and the second one in Panther Brook Glen.

Helm had the silver assayed out and found that it was an unusually pure strain of silver. He was well paid for his good deed. However, Helm wanted more. He began to walk the areas of Shohola Glen and Panther Brook Glen looking for an entrance, but he never found one.

Helm eventually took an Indian woman as his wife. He hoped that this act of fidelity would cement his relationship with the natives, and they would confide the secret location to him. But his marriage did not profit him as he had hoped. For most of her life his wife kept her people's secret. Upon her death bed she revealed that she had been threatened by her people with a terrible death if she spoke to any white man about the silver mine. It was not until Helm's wife was dying that she tried to tell him the location of the mine, but then she was too ill to talk much. She was unable to impart to Holm's the location he so desperately sought.

After her death, Helm spent the rest of his life searching in vain for the mine or cave that the chief had once shown him. He would never again find it.

As the area grew more populated, folks began to laugh at the old man. The Indians were driven from the land, and so were the tales of their treasure. However, all of that changed when in 1884 an Indian from the Cattaraugus Reservation came the town of Sweden Valley. He walked into the woods there and returned a few hours later with five pounds of pure silver ore. The man seemed to be coming from Ice Mountain. Within the year, the Indian came again from the reservation and returned once more with pure silver ore. From time to time, men from the reservation returned to the area and left with several pounds of raw silver ore. Although, there were several attempts to follow the Indian man, no one was ever successful.

Through the years, those who have searched for the silver cave have come to a few conclusions. They believe that the cave can only be accessed by a slit in the side of the mountain, and that a similar slit or crack in the mountain offers access to the cave from the other side as well. One entrance must be in Panther Brook Glen, and the other one must be accessible from Shohola Glen. There was an Indian trail that crossed between the two glens and many believe that this trail was placed there by natives traveling through between the two paths that lead into the mountainside.

There is no doubt that silver bullets and arrows came from that area long ago. But anyone looking for the silver cave would have to be most patient and methodical and more than a little lucky.

MICHAEL RIZ Z ALO
(Luzerne County)

Michael Rizzalo (also spelled Rizzolo in the newspaper accounts) sat at the defendant's table and listened as his attorney, John Garman, laid out before the jury several different scenarios as to how he came to be involved in the payroll robbery of a local lumber company. Michael Rizzalo sat and listened as the owner of the lumber company testified that he had commissioned a paymaster named McClure to bring the twelve thousand dollar payroll with him by train to pay the men. Then others took up the story and told of how Michael Rizzalo, Vincent Valalli and Guiseppe Benevino had stolen the payroll and shot Paymaster McClure and his companion named Flanagan.

Michael Rizzalo, an Italian immigrant, knew that his two cohorts in crime were far beyond the reach of the Luzerne County Prosecution. They were back in Italy where they had fled after the robbery and murder. Ironically, Michael had taken charge of the payroll money and had hidden it where only he knew of its existence. His two fellow criminals were virtually penniless after their big haul.

Michael Rizzalo was a short, beefy man who had worked at various menial jobs since arriving in America. He spoke broken English with a thick accent and was known by his cohorts as "Red-nosed Mike" because he was a heavy drinker.

Mike was terrified as he sat there. His very life lay on the line. He didn't understand all of the rules that had been explained to him, but he did understand that he was facing a death sentence. Attorney Garman seemed to be struggling with the case. He was a competent attorney who had tried in many ways to mitigate things for Rizzalo, but had failed at every turn.

The robbery and murder had made nearly every newspaper in the state and had been big news in Wilkes-Barre and the surrounding area. There were few who could read who had not devoured the newspaper stories of the Rizzalo and his criminal buddies. Even those who could not read had heard the story, and most everyone had already formed an opinion on the case. Attorney Garman had asked for a change of venue, but that had been denied.

Among those who testified that day was police Captain Linden who had arrested Rizzalo. He testified that Rizzalo had confessed to the shooting death of Paymaster McClure and Flanagan, and that he had said that he had been forced to commit the crime by a local acquaintance and thug named Guiseppe Benevino.

In the end, despite Attorney John Garman's various attempts to mitigate things, Michael Rizzalo would be found guilty of murder in the first degree. He was sentenced on April 29, 1889 to be executed for the murders. Attorney Garman had failed to convince the jury that Rizzalo was either an innocent bystander or that he had been coerced into the crime by his buddy, Guiseppe Benevino.

Michael Rizzalo was executed on June 25, 1889 without having revealed any more information about the whereabouts of the payroll.

Benevino and Valalli would later be caught and brought back to America. Both men would always insist that Michael Rizzalo had hidden the tin box containing the twelve thousand dollars in payroll. Michael Rizzalo insisted that he had hidden the money somewhere on Laurel Run Creek, about four miles from Wilkes-Barre, but the money never turned up. Michael Rizzalo took the truth of the murders and the secret of the money to his grave.

Today it is impossible to estimate how much the payroll money would be worth. There are many factors that would come into play. What condition the money was in, the types and denominations of the bills and other factors could vastly change the estimates. But there is little doubt that if the money could be found, and linked to Rizzalo and his cohorts, it would create a sensation and could possibly make someone quite wealthy.

THE LOST FRANKLIN LIBRARY
(Philadelphia County)

Throughout this book, I have attempted to offer up not only the standard fare of buried pirate's gold, but more unique treasures as well. Years ago a friend of mine purchased at a yard sale an old painting that just appealed to him. My friend took the picture home, but had a "feeling" about it. He did some research and found that there was an interesting story in the painting. It turned out that the painting was by a little-known, but highly collectable, artist from the early twentieth century. The painting had cost him five dollars and was worth nearly a thousand dollars. It is also the premise of shows such as The Antiques Road Show that one man's trash can be another man's treasure. I have always loved and revered books and can not bear to see a tome destroyed. To that end, I've collected quite a few "worthless" books that I have later learned did have a financial value. As a bibliophile, I could not resist this story of a most amazing and unique treasure in Pennsylvania.

The life of Benjamin Franklin was more amazing than any fictional novel ever written. Who would believe that a child who only attended school until the age of ten could grow up to become one of the most influential people in the history of the world. He would become a writer, businessman, politician, philosopher, and scientist. His words and wisdom are as applicable in today's society as when he penned the words over two hundred years ago. Every day Benjamin Franklin's legacy touches our lives. He created the first public library and fire department in America. He started the Post office in this nation and discovered that electricity was a force that could be controlled and used for the public good. He created bifocals and one of the most efficient heating stoves ever known. He could have made many fortunes with his scientific inventions, but he gave them all to the public for free.

Benjamin Franklin was himself a bibliophile, or collector of books. He was a voracious reader who sought to learn all that he could. His library of reading material was vast and varied. He owned copies of Latin texts and scientific and medical tomes such as works by Sir Isaac Newton. But he also owned classics such as Don Quixote, technical manuals, and even a book on the making of apple cider. In all, it is estimated that Benjamin Franklin's library housed 4,276 volumes, and it is known that he built an addition to his home in Philadelphia to house the massive collection.

However, when Benjamin Franklin died 1790, he left the vast majority of his book collection to his grandson, William Templeton Franklin who apparently did not share his grandfather's love of books. William Templeton Franklin saw the books as a problem and had them warehoused until he could figure out what to do with them. In the end, he decided to sell them for a profit. His famous grandfather's books were sold to Robert Morris Jr. who would go bankrupt four years later. During that trying time Morris sold the books to a bookseller named Nicholas Dufief. Dufief subsequently began to parcel out the books to clients from 1801 until 1803. Among his clients was the then President, Thomas Jefferson who also bought some of Franklin's library. At one point, the young Library of Congress attempted to purchase the remainder of the Franklin's library so that it would not be lost to history, but the deal fell through.

And this is what brings us to the mystery of this library collection. Although Franklin had a complete catalog of his books made, it no longer survives. Furthermore, the catalog of the books sold to Dufief by Templeton Franklin also was destroyed. Amazingly, even the catalogs of the books for sale by Dufief has been lost to historians and bibliophiles. This means that no one knows for sure exactly how many books Franklin actually did own or where they might have gone. Various books were bequeathed to specific people and institutions upon Franklin's death. Those would not be listed on Templeton Franklin's list, but would have been on Benjamin Franklin's private list of books. Furthermore, it is not known exactly where many of the privately owned books have gone. But there are tantalizing clues that could help a treasure hunter find the books.

In 1935, members of the American Philosophical Society, a group founded by Franklin, noticed that in the volumes of Franklin's books they had purchased from Dufief there was a curious marking. It was a "shelf mark" which had been placed in the book to help with locating the book for future reference. As the Philosophical Society did not use such marks, either Dufief or Franklin must have placed the mark in the books because they all had it. The mark was quite distinctive. It was a penciled marking inside the cover of each book. It was a letter "C" followed by numbers and then a letter "N" followed by further numbers. But the question of who made the marks and what they stood for would be very important to the mystery of the missing books.

It would be a hotly debated question among bibliophiles until 1956 when a librarian from another of the institutions that Benjamin Franklin had started long ago solved part of the mystery. Edwin Wolf, a librarian at the Library Company, which had been started in 1731 by Benjamin Franklin and friends, found proof that several volumes had been bequeathed directly to the Library Company and to the Philosophical Society, and that these books, too, had the markings. This meant that Benjamin Franklin must have placed the markings in the books since these volumes had gone directly from Franklin's collection into the hands of the societies that still owned them. Dufief had never seen nor handled those volumes. This discovery meant that there was now a clear and concise way to tell if a book really was from the Franklin library. Furthermore, Wolf poured over the vast amount of letters that Franklin had written and found that in the letters he mentioned owning over 700 books that were not yet found. Wolf would also discover that some "unmarked" books actually had the "shelf mark" but it had been covered over by face plates from subsequent owners, erased by later owners, or had been covered over when volumes were rebound. That made the task of finding the precious Franklin volumes even more difficult.

In 1962, a decedent of Benjamin Franklin Bache came forward with further information. Benjamin Franklin Bache was another of Franklin's grandson's and he had been left a smaller collection of books by his grandfather. His descendants found among his papers an inventory of titles in the handwriting of Templeton Franklin. In it the "C" and "N" were explained by

Templeton. It turns out that the "C" stands for Case and the "N" for number. The information was used by Benjamin Franklin to reference where he'd find a book on his shelves. This information was then registered beside each title so that Franklin could look at his inventory and locate a book quickly. It functioned much like our card catalog system does today. This document was the final proof that Benjamin Franklin, not Dufief, had marked the books.

In 1991, Mr. Wolf died leaving behind an inventory of books from the Franklin library that he believed consisted of only one fourth of the books in the total library. Subsequently, teacher and researcher, Kevin Hayes, has continued the work. The dream of historians and bibliophiles is to completely restore the entire Franklin library. It is a daunting task, but it would serve a purpose. A complete library of Franklin's books would be valuable to historians as they research Franklin's work. It would explain his mindset and point of view and help them to sharpen their understanding of this most amazing man.

Sadly, it is probably impossible to completely restore Franklin's vast library. Through the years, books have doubtlessly been destroyed. Furthermore, other books might never come to light as having belonged to Benjamin Franklin. However, each volume that is added is another piece of the historical puzzle that is so valuable to historians, authors and teachers.

Today it is known that many of Benjamin Franklin's books are scattered throughout Pennsylvania, New Jersey, Delaware and Washington D.C. However, volumes could literally have traveled anywhere in the world. The Historical Society of Pennsylvania, the Philosophical Society and the Library Company own the vast majority of Benjamin Franklin's known books. What has happened to the remaining books is a true mystery. Anyone who finds a book of Benjamin Franklin's, that can be authenticated, could be very wealthy. Such a book could be sold for a great deal, and it would be welcomed by those who have dedicated their lives to understanding Benjamin Franklin. Though this is an unconventional treasure, it is certainly an amazing one, and a treasure that can be hunted in old book stores, yard sales and flea markets among other places.

A vigilant person could unearth not just a treasure for themselves, but a treasure for the nation.

THE AUGUSTA AND MERLIN
(Philadelphia County)

During the American Revolutionary War, the British Government never faltered in its belief that it would win back the recalcitrant colonies. After all, the British were a conquering people. They had claimed many other lands for themselves around the world. What the British government was not prepared to factor in was that the "colonials" were just as determined to win. At the beginning of the war the British looked upon the whole thing as a nuisance that had to be squelched. The colonials were an ungrateful lot who didn't appreciate the fact that the British government had just paid a fortune out to protect the colonists during the French and Indian wars. The nonsense over taxation would surely die away. Why shouldn't the British crown tax the colonials to help pay the bill for protecting them?

But as things progressed, the British military realized that the colonials were going to be formidable opponents. The British military officers realized that the best way to win the war was to reclaim the cities and to isolate the colonials. To that end, they secured several major cities. First they secured New York, and then British General Sir William Howe went on to defeat General Washington and the colonial army at White Plains on October 28, 1776. Howe had sent his opponents on the run back into Pennsylvania and he was determined to pursue them. He believed, however, that one place he'd need to secure was Philadelphia which was a major port. The psychological victory of this would go a long way toward winning the war. He knew that he'd never really win Philadelphia unless he could gain control of the port once more. To do that he needed the help of his brother, Admiral Richard Howe who was commanding the fleet in the region.   A campaign to take back Philadelphia began. Admiral Richard Howe transported the armed forces to the Chesapeake Bay to where they landed and attacked Philadelphia. The American's loss at Brandywine on September 11, 1777 allowed General William Howe to take back Philadelphia. That done, he set his sites on controlling the Delaware River and the port at Philadelphia. The Howe Brothers knew that they were facing a formidable problem. The river was guarded by underwater obstacles called "Chevaux-de-frise." There were also two forts standing in the way of victory for the British. Forts Mercer and Mifflin were going to have to fall in order for the British to regain control of the water way. A combined land and water attack of both forts was planned for mid-October of 1777.

The British fleet bombarded both forts, and on October 22, 1777 Fort Mifflin faced attack by the British Fleet. During the battle the *HMS Augusta* and *HMS Merlin* were destroyed. The *HMS Merlin* ran aground in the shallows during an engagement with American gun batteries. Both ships found themselves facing a terrible barrage of fire from Fort Mifflin and American warships. The *HMS Merlin* was so badly damaged that it was abandoned and sunk as a total loss. The *HMS Augusta* burst into flames and exploded. It is said that at the time of their loss, both war ships had been carrying approximately two million dollars in gold and silver coin that was headed to Germantown to pay troops there. The treasure was never recovered to the best of anyone's knowledge. The remnants of the *HMS Augusta* were visible for many years after the battle while the *HMS Merlin* was submerged. In that same year, a map of the river was made which showed the sinking sites for both ships. However, none of the gold and silver was ever salvaged.

It would be easy to dismiss the story as untrue except for the fact that in 1866, workers of the Tomlinson Dredging Company first glimpsed what they thought was a treasure chest. It took years before they could bring up the chest, but in 1897 the chest was finally raised. It was found to be a brass-bound trunk full of gold and silver coins. There was no positive link between it and the two ships, but it was found in the area where they went down. The amount in the trunk was only a small portion of what is believed to be under water awaiting discovery. It would be an amazing find if anyone ever was to discover it. What seems true, is that a vast fortune in gold and silver is under the Delaware River awaiting the soul who can find it and bring it up. By now it is most assuredly covered by layers of silt and sand. The treasure very well could have shifted, but a study of the currents and tides in the area could be a great help in tracing this fortune.

Throughout October and into November Fort Mifflin and Fort Mercer were under attack. On November 16, 1777 Fort Mifflin did fall to the British. For some time the British controlled the waterways but, in the end, it did them little good. For the one foe that the British could not defeat were their own brothers. In the struggle for independence both sides neglected the fortune under the waters. It would have been nearly impossible to bring it to the surface at the time, and so the story of the *HMS Merlin* and *HMS Augusta* became the stuff of legends. Except that perhaps someone will find the treasures still.

THE LAKE ERIE GRAVEYARD
OF SHIPS
(Erie County)

Today we recognize that where there are busy shipping lanes there are many wrecks. The media has popularized the idea of the Bermuda Triangle--Graveyard of Ships; a place where uncanny events have led to bizarre accidents and strange disappearances of both ships and aircraft. But what most folks don't realize is that Pennsylvania is edged by a lake that is known to be more dangerous than the Bermuda Triangle, and that this lake has swallowed a vast array of ships and planes through the years. This waterway has been dubbed "Lake Erie's Graveyard of Ships" and is located in the "Great Lakes Triangle."

It would take a separate volume to chronicle exactly what has been happening on Lake Erie, but we'll give a brief overview. The Great Lakes are known for their dangerous, unpredictable waters and murky depths. The water is cold and that adds another layer of danger for divers and salvagers. Lake Erie, as with all the Great Lakes, is a busy waterway that sees a great deal of ship traffic even today. Travel by water has always been popular and convenient in the Lake Erie area, but it has always come at a cost. I've decided to go into a few of the most important wrecks in Lake Erie one by one because there are so many of them. By no means are these all of the wrecks, nor does this include the various plane wrecks that have also happened over the Lake. It is just an overview of some of the most interesting wrecks from the prospective of treasure hunting.

In 1721, a French frigate christened the *Le Jean Florin* sailed across Lake Erie. It was the second of July and the waters were calm. It should have been an easy passage, but approximately fifteen miles east of Erie something went wrong and the ship sank. Among the items in the cargo that day was over five hundred thousand dollars in gold coins and silver bullion. None of the gold nor any relics have ever been recovered from this ship.

There are several unknown wrecks in the lake off the city of Erie. The cargo carried by several of the vessels is unknown, but there have long been reports that gold species are among the salvageable artifacts in the area. Nothing from the wrecks has ever been salvaged according to reports.

There have long been stories of Spanish gold in Lake Erie, and these stories were substantiated when a dredger captain made an amazing discovery in the mid-1900's. The captain dredged up Spanish pieces-of-eight minted in 1698. The coins were found lying atop a pile of sand spit out by the dredger. They are certainly proof that some sort of Spanish gold might be in the lake waiting to be recovered. The captain had been forced to move his dredger because it was encountering an underwater obstacle that might have snared his hose. Could that "obstacle" have been the ship?

The sloop *Detroit* sank about three miles north of Erie in 1797. The cargo aboard the ship were military supplies and a probable payroll of gold coins. Nothing has ever been recovered from this wreck.

The steamer *Atlantic* went down on August 19, 1852 with a strong box carrying a sum between three hundred thousand dollars and sixty thousand dollars in gold in the ship's large safe. Four years later a strong box supposed to be from that wreck was recovered, but there was only thirty-six thousand dollars in it. This leaves a vast fortune in gold unaccounted for. Nothing further was ever recovered from the wreck of the *Atlantic,* including the ship's safe.

When the *Young Sion* went down on June 12, 1881, it was carrying iron for the railroad and gold coins. The amount of money on board was never determined, but it is known that the ship was carrying a quantity of gold. The ship went down about two miles out from Walnut Creek and that would place it west of the city of Erie.

The cargo aboard the *Dean Richmond* included one hundred forty-one thousand dollars in gold and over fifty thousand dollars in zinc bars. The ship went down on August 19, 1893, about two miles north of Erie and was never recovered. It is estimated that she lies in about 140 feet of water today. Coast Guard charts would help determine exactly where it lies and how to approach it.

The waters off the city of Girard are laden with shipwrecks and the salvage from them could be very lucrative. The *Dundee* went down on September 11, 1900 carrying iron ore. It is estimated that it would value out at about twenty thousand dollars in salvage. The *John B. Lyon,* a freighter, also sank on September 11, 1900, about four miles north east of Girard. It would be worthwhile to find it for salvage rights. The *F.A. Georger* sank about four miles out from Girard carrying over one hundred thousand dollars in iron. Today the salvage value for this iron would be immense.

Just off the coast of the city of Erie, the steamer *Erie* went down with twenty thousand dollars in gold on board. It was never found and could be salvaged. But the story of the *Erie* is a tragic one. It is a graveyard of sorts for those who went down with her.

Throughout the years, a few gold and silver coins have been discovered near Lawrence Park along the Lake Erie shore. The only explanation for how the coins came to be there is that they have washed up from old ship wrecks.

The wrecks listed above are only a few of the many

wrecks in Lake Erie. Most of them would be worth something as salvage, but a large number of the wrecks were known to be carrying metals such as gold, silver, zinc and iron. The price for these metals today would certainly make them worthwhile if they could be found. Of course, it is not that simple or else someone would have done so by now. The fact of the matter is that Lake Erie is a dangerous place. The currents are swift, storms can blow up suddenly, and the water is cold and murky. Visibility in the silt laden water is practically zero at times, and it would take intense work to find the wrecks and a great deal of money to bring them up. The problem for most folks is that they simply lack the funds necessary to pull off such a large operation until the wreck is found and the pay off is made. Furthermore, a person would have to file for salvage rights and be sure that the U.S. Government or someone else does not already hold those rights. For those reasons the wrecks are still there awaiting the day when someone will find them and bring up the riches on board.

THE SECRET OF UNIONTOWN
(Fayette County)

Is it possible that a fortune in silver bars or ingots could be hidden in a cave near Uniontown, and that most of the fortune is still there? As strange as that sounds, there is some evidence to indicate that perhaps such a thing is possible.

According to old stories, there are fifteen tons of silver bars hidden in a cave outside of Uniontown, but nothing about this story comes easy. Everything is clouded in the mists of time, and there are two different versions of how the lost treasure came about.

The oldest story took place during the War of 1812, when the British made a futile attempt to get back the United States by battle. It is said that during the war, a load of silver was being transported by ox cart from Buffalo, New York to Washington D.C. But when the British took Washington D.C., the silver was hidden in a cave along the way rather than risk that it would fall into the hands of the British. Why it was never recovered it not known.

The second story runs along the same lines except that the war has changed. According to the second version of the story, the silver was being transported by train when it was robbed by Confederate sympathizers or Confederate soldiers in 1865 just before the end of the war. The silver was too heavy to carry far, and so it was secreted in a cave by the Confederates for future retrieval. But when the South surrendered, the silver bars were lost in the shuffle and eventually forgotten about. Why those who buried it did not return for it is unknown, but there are several possible reasons. The Confederates or Confederate sympathizers could have feared being found out and arrested. The thieves could have died or been unable to return for various reasons. It is merely speculation, though, as to why a vast fortune would be allowed to gather dust in a remote Pennsylvania cave.

However it came to be there, the silver has long been rumored to be hidden in a cave outside of Uniontown. This could simply be considered a legend except for a few facts that lend credence to the reality of the silver.

It is said that in 1957, two hunters stumbled upon the cave and explored it. They found the silver inside and realized that they had found a vast fortune. The two men were afraid that the U.S. Government would confiscate the treasure if anyone confessed to knowing about it, so instead they let it in the cave and decided to slowly siphon off a little money at a time. But human nature being what it is, they decided that it would be better to move the money to a "safer" place, and so they decided to move it to an old abandoned mine they knew. The job would have been arduous and daunting, but supposedly they did move the silver bars.

Interestingly, silver ingots have turned up in Pennsylvania, Ohio, and Illinois. The ingots weigh three and a half pounds and are stamped with the words:

"Syracuse Smelting Works
Government Genuine
New York City"

The reverse side is stamped with **"Alloyed under the Stanley process"** which could help date the ingots.

The existence of these ingots lends credibility to the tale, but there are still a lot of questions unanswered. Why didn't the hunters ever spend any of the loot? How did the people who own the ingots come into possession of them? Why have they never retrieved the loot? Strange as it sounds, there is a secret hidden in the caves and old mines around Uniontown, and the person who unravels the secret could become very wealthy indeed.

DIAMONDS IN THE SKY
(Venango County)
November 22, 1928

In the early 1900's planes were only beginning to see their potential. Forward thinkers saw great potential in them but many others did not. There was a running argument that planes were not safe. That when they malfunctioned it was much more dangerous than when a car did. Some people believed that flying as a practical part of every day life was foolishness, but the cause of planes in practical use got a big boost when the U.S. Post Office began an air mail service. Those planes carried tons of mail around the nation and did so efficiently and effectively, but like all things mechanical, planes did malfunction from time to time.

The pilot glanced at the instrument panel in desperation one more time. The instrument readings only confirmed what he already knew. The plane was in deep trouble. The pilot was flying an officially sanctioned U.S. Postal Service airmail plane and he had made this same run many times before. But on that day, everything had gone suddenly very wrong.

The sputtering of the plane as it died out froze the man's heart. He was rapidly loosing control of the situation and his options were growing more limited by the second. He had to find a place to set the plane down that was not populated, and hopefully he could find a field to land in. His eyes desperately scanned the terrain below, but he saw no hope. All there were were mountains and woods as far as he could see. Little clusters of houses broke the monotony of the scenery and the pilot's heart sank with each second. He was going down and it wouldn't be good. He was going to have to try and bring the plane down in the forest. It was a virtual death sentence and he knew it, but he chose to keep the plane over unpopulated territory. He could live with his own death but he couldn't bear to think that he would be taking others with him.

The pilot watched as the earth seemed to suddenly rush up toward him. He knew that in reality it was the plane rushing downward as gravity made it plummet. He braced for the impact and heard the ripping as the plane struck the trees. He felt the impact of the first contact with the unyielding forest, and then the secondary crash as the trees did yield by tearing into the plane and spilling the contents out behind him. The mail looked like confetti streaming out as it smashed into the ground. There was silence and the pilot did not make it out of the plane.

The plane had been over Bear Hollow near the town of Polk, and not far from Oil City when it began to experience problems. The plane had gone down in Bear Hollow, and it was there that the confetti of mail was found along with the wreckage and the pilot.

The cargo of mail bags were found on the ground and some of them were severely damaged by heat and the impact, but there was a package among the cargo that was of special interest to Postal Inspector Bill Tafel who secured the crash site. Tafel treated the site more like a crime scene and set many of the locals to wondering what was really going on at the crash site. Within an hour of the crash, Tafel had arrived and sealed up the site. He had brought guards with him who circled the area and refused to let any civilians in. He then pushed past the reporters and ordered everyone out of the area. What Tafel knew was that the plane had been carrying eleven hundred unset diamonds for dealers to pick up in the mid-west. The packages were ruptured when found and the diamonds were scattered over a large part of the crash area.

Postal workers were sent in from Pittsburgh and a painstaking search began. In fact, some have labeled it the largest diamond hunt in North America. With Tafel in the lead, the postal employees searched and sifted every inch of the crash area. Searchers were eventually able to find seven hundred twenty-five diamonds, but that left a fortune in unset stones unaccounted for. Among the missing gems was a nine-carat stone worth more than eighteen thousand dollars at that time. Today the value would have multiplied many times over.

Despite the best searches conducted by the U.S. Postal Service Inspector Bill Tafel, the gems remain unaccounted for. It would be a painstaking search and would literally have to be conducted like one were panning for gold, but finding those diamonds could be lucrative. Of course, the proper officials would have to be notified for the diamonds were insured, but a finders fee or some sort of fee could well apply. It would certainly be interesting to see some of those diamonds appear. Their history might actually make them all the more appealing to the buyers. After all, who doesn't love a great story attached to a precious stone

WHAT A PENNY'S WORTH?
(Mifflin County)

Okay, so we all know that a penny is not worth much these days. Only in a few isolated country stores are there even those jars of penny candy that so many of us took for granted when we were young--and some of us remember when a penny might buy you two red jelly fish or three tootsie rolls. However, there is a story of a train robbery from Lewistown, Mifflin County that proves that even today a penny can still hold its value.

Train engineer Sam Donnelly wiped the sweat from his neck with a crumpled, stained red bandana and tucked it back in his pocket. It was 1:30 a.m. on August 31st of 1909, and the heat of the day seemed to have seeped into the darkness. It was made worse from the heat inside the train car where he stood. A cool night breeze occasionally flickered in the window of the

Pittsburgh & Northern Express train Engine #39 that he was driving. Behind him cars rattled on the tracks in rhythm with the jiggling of Engine #39. Among the cars he was pulling were the cars that belonged to Adams Express. Adams Express cars carried vast quantities of cash for banks and businesses up and down the line, but Donnelly barely gave the vast fortune behind him a thought because he carried such cars on nearly every one of his nightly runs.

There were only two other men with him on this run. Usually there was one more man aboard the freight express, but the man who worked for Adams Express had taken ill and had not come to work. Donnelly didn't think much about the missing fellow because there had never been an incident aboard the trains.

He slowed the train a bit as it entered a narrow gap in the terrain made by the edge of Black Log Mountain on one side and the Juniata River and the canal on the other. This spot was known locally as the Lewistown Narrows, and through the center of it ran the all-important railroad.

Suddenly the darkness erupted with noise. An explosion rocked the train. Donnelly jammed the brake hard, and then released it. Repeatedly, he worked the mechanism until the train drew to a stop. As he worked, more explosions seemed to rock the train. Something was drastically wrong and he suspected that something inside of Engine #39 was exploding.

In the darkness, Sam Donnelly jumped down to the ground as the train drew to a stop. He heard the familiar voice of the conductor, Mr. Poffenberger and the sound of the brakeman's shout. They were getting off the train, too. The three men had just met near the side of Engine #39 when gunfire ripped through the night and a lone man stepped forward from the darkness. The man was short and he wore a burlap sack over most of his body. The eyeholes gleamed in the darkness and a big, black hat completed the strange disguise. The man would have looked comical if not for the revolver in each hand that he had already proved he could shoot, and the sticks of dynamite that protruded from his pockets.

"Move," the bandit growled, pointing with a gun back along the line of train cars. The three men stared for long seconds until the bandit ripped off another shot in their direction. "I said move."

The three men began to walk back the line of train cars. At the first Adams Express car the thief paused only a second. "Not that one," he muttered more to himself than the frightened men. He moved on and dismissed another car from Adams Express. He paused before yet another one and this time he forced the brakeman to open the door. As he prepared to leap aboard the car, there was a sudden flurry of activity. Poffenberger had grabbed a brake club and had swung it in the direction of the thief. The thief seemed to somehow anticipate the attack and turned as he fired a shot into Poffenberger's hand. The wounded conductor dropped the brake club and fell to his knees. The pain in his hand was intense, but he made no sound.

With a sudden leap that warned the men that this thief was quite muscular, the man vaulted into the now open train car. He never left them, but rather began grabbing up bags of money with one hand and chucking them out the doorway while he kept a revolver trained on them with the other.

He tossed the moneybags marked for Adams Express onto the ground with a clink that told the men that he was stealing coins of some sort. When he had thrown several heavy bags down, the bandit took a single leap back to the ground.

With quiet efficiency that warned the men that this robbery had been planned out, the thief kicked at the nearest bag. "Pick them up," he hissed. The men bent over and grabbed up the bags of coins. Even Poffenberger was forced to pick up bags of coins and carry them.

"Walk," the thief pointed back toward the darkness.

The three men stumbled through the darkness in the direction that the thief had indicated. At the edge of the tree line the men found an opening that turned into a trail. The heavy burden of the coins and their own reluctance slowed the men down as they began the long trek that they soon realized was a climb up Black Log Mountain.

At one point the thief, who seemed quite silent, became impatient with the progress of the men. He fired a couple shots over their heads and ordered them to hurry. The hostages obliged, but it was growing increasingly obvious that

Poffenberger was faltering.

At last the thief paused and ordered them to put some of the money down. He decided what money should be left behind and ordered the men to once again resume their climb.

Again their progress grew slow and he once more decided which money he would not take. Again a few small bags were left on the trial.

At last the men were ordered for the final time to put the money down. Then the thief ordered them back down the mountain and, as an added incentive, once again shot at the retreating men.

Soon word spread that there had been a train robbery at the Lewistown Narrows. The Adams Express agent was accused of the robbery but was eventually cleared. The Express Company announced that the thief had made off with $5,049.00 in gold and $100 in silver dollars. He had also taken two $100 bags of newly minted Lincoln head pennies. The theft of the pennies seemed like an accident, and no one thought much about it.

Within hours Pinkerton agents, local police, and a pack of bloodhounds that had been shipped in from the Baltimore & Ohio Railroad were on the trail.

Here the story begins to fall apart. In one account most of the money was recovered, though the thief was never found. Another account does not mention the money being recovered, and it was believed that he had stashed the loot before making off along a mountain trail that led into Maryland. In yet another account, he tossed away or stashed only the pennies and the rest of the money was taken away.

There was rank speculation that the thief was James Lawler, a well-known robber. Other folks insisted that James would never have committed such a daring robbery without his cohort and brother, John. This argument was used to both prove that the Lawler brothers were guilty and to prove that they were not. After all, not once did anyone mention seeing a second man.

No horse droppings were ever found, and so many of the police surmised that the thief or thieves, as the case may have been, had actually walked off the mountain. To this day, no one actually knows for sure who the robber was, however, many accounts assume it was James, John or both brothers who committed the crime.

The money was eventually recovered, except for some of the pennies. There was a total of $65 in pennies that were never recovered. However, in 1953, three deer hunters stumbled over 3,700 pennies in rotting Adams Express bags. The money was found about half a mile east of the village of Hawstone. Today 2,800 pennies have yet to be recovered.

As treasures go, that might seem like a pittance. However collectors and treasure hunters believe that the pennies are worth between $3 and $500 each depending upon their mintmarks and quality. It is believed that a quantity of rare, newly minted 1909 VDB-S pennies were among the coins that are still missing. That would make the total fortune yet to be found in the woods of Lewistown Narrows worth between $8,400 and $1,400,000. Now, what is a penny worth?

SO WHAT ARE THE ODDS?

If so much treasure and loot is actually missing in Pennsylvania, then why hasn't any of it been found? The truth is that some of it has been found, but those stories were not well publicized. Through the years, there are stories of vast fortunes and strange finds that lend credence to the idea that Pennsylvania is home to mysterious fortunes and regal relics. Consider the following tales before you close this book and give up on the idea of treasure hunting.

Sunken Slot Machines

It is easy to be seduced by the lore of sunken treasure ships. People think of stories like that of Mel Fischer and the

Atocha. But Pennsylvania has many sunken treasure stories. Lake Erie has lost more than its share of ships and it is actually an area where treasure divers actively seek loot. Pennsylvania born diver Burt Webber found a Spanish galleon, the *Conception,* at Silver Banks and became famous. But Burt began his treasure diving career by diving for sunken slot machines in the quarries near his home town of Annville in Lebanon County. He salvaged the machines for a profit. There is great truth in the old adage that one man's junk is another man's treasure, and Burt Webber has made a good living at it.

Dump Site Gold Cache

Near Chadd's Ford, the police found the body of seventy-four year old Katherine Wood dumped in a secluded area. Ms. Wood was the victim of foul play, and while searching the site the police stumbled over an unexpected find. They collected twenty thousand dollars in coins from the woods. There was no indication of where the cache came from.

The Cave Loot

In Wyoming County in 1975, a treasure hunter set out to find an old cave rumored to be the site where gold and silver coins were hidden that dated back to the early 1800's. The story was that in the Endless Mountains near Nicholson, there was supposed to be a cave where a treasure of chests of gold and silver coins was hidden. The story was popularized by an old shoemaker who showed a few gold coins as proof of his tale, but he never sold the coins and never got wealthy.

In modern times, a treasure hunter decided that he'd set out to look for the cave in a loop around the Nicholson area and would continue outward looking for caves in hopes of finding the right one. To his delight, he did find a cave that contained a treasure. In a cave he found two little buckets and fourteen old tobacco cans full of silver and copper coins. However, the coins bore U.S. mint marks and dates that precluded them from being the treasure that the shoemaker had talked about. Still, the find was quite exciting for the treasure hunter and he certainly got more than many folks do when they begin searching for treasure. There are no reports about the value of the coins that the treasure hunter found.

Treasure Chest

Treasure hunting is often a matter of persistence and for a group of treasure hunters in the 1970's, persistence paid off. The group was hunting a treasure rumored to be in the Warrior's Run area of Luzerne County. It is not believed that they found that treasure, but they did indeed find a treasure chest with an unexpected pay off.

The group were working in the Haystack Mountain area where an old Civilian Conservation Corp Camp (known commonly as C.C.C. camps) had once been. The C.C.C. camps were work camps created by the Franklin Roosevelt administration to offer jobs to young men. The men and boys were recruited to work on building roads, improving parks and other forestry work. In exchange, the boys got three meals, clothes and valuable training. They'd also received a small stipend, but the majority of their pay would go back to their families. It was a program that helped many families and shaped many young lives. The mountains of Pennsylvania are today riddled with such abandoned facilities. It was at the C.C.C. on Haystack Mountain where they made their discovery. In one of the abandoned buildings of the old camp they found a chestnut chest filled with jewelry hidden in the rotting walls of the old building. Where it came from and how it got there will probably never be known, but clearly someone was hoarding a treasure as the Great Depression roared across this nation. It is not known how much the jewelry was sold for, but it is believed that this find has nothing to do with a local story about a treasure known as the "Warrior Gap Treasure." This treasure would have been much older than that found at the C.C.C. camp.

The Silver Bar

A group of hikers in 1977 were taking a walk through the woods of Warren County near Smithfield when one of their number saw something strange. It looked like something oblong was wedged in the crack between two rocks on a hillside. He drew the attention of the group to the strange item and they decided to inspect it further. The group climbed the hill and pried the object loose. To their surprise it was a bar of solid silver. The hikers took it to the proper authorities who attempted to discover how it had come to be there. In the end, it was decided that the bar was from a long lost treasure rumored to have been lost in the area. If the theory is accurate, then it is only the first tantalizing clue to a vast fortune waiting to be discovered.

Digging Up Gold

Digging fern roots sounds like a fairly innocent occupation and it usually is, but for two men in 1884 it led them to digging up unbelievable riches. The two men were digging on a small island south of Danville when they struck something hard. They unearthed a chest and broke it open. What was inside was like something from a pirate movie. There was forty-seven thousand dollars in gold and silver coinage. Part of the loot was Spanish gold! There were no local stories to explain how the gold and silver came to be buried there. Local speculation at the time was that it was a pirate's treasure that had been secreted there in the long ago.

Cleaning House

Imagine the surprise that a family in Huntingdon had when they decided to clean out the basement of their home in the Petersburg area. While cleaning up, the family found several jars of old coins. At first the jars of old coins didn't look like much, but when they were gathered together and counted, they totaled almost fourteen hundred dollars. Better yet, the coins were in good condition and dated from the 1920's through the 1930's. Some of the coins were worth many times their face value. It was a great way to clean up while cleaning out their old basement.

What's a Treasure

What exactly constitutes a treasure? A treasure is something that you can find of value in my estimation. In that case, there are divers in Lake Erie who are treasure hunting for a most unusual treasure--wood. Ships carrying prime lumber sank years ago leaving their loads at the bottom of the lake. Today that wood is often considered very valuable. There are salvage companies that specialize in raising the lumber and then marketing it. Granted, this is not what you typically think of as treasure, but logs worth thousands of dollars are quite lucrative for those men.

Mexican Gold

There have long been rumors of Spanish or Mexican gold buried in Huntingdon County, but most folks just scoffed at the old legends. However, Spain did once show a great deal of interest in the county. Imagine the surprise that workers had in 1886 when they were digging a water reservoir at the end of 5th Street. The men came across an iron pot filled with Mexican and early American gold and silver coins. How the gold got there, who had buried it and what happened to it after it was discovered is not known. But the fact that the gold was found seems to indicate that those old rumors and legends deserve a second look.

Sunken Gold

Along the Delaware River there have been finds of Spanish gold doubloons that are believed to be part of a treasure ship sunken long ago.

Near Lawrence Park on the shores of Lake Erie, silver and gold coins have been found. It is believed that these old coins were washed ashore from one of the many wrecks in the lake. People today do not realize it, but Lake Erie has claimed more ships than the Bermuda Triangle and there are vast fortunes laying beneath the murky waters of all of the Great Lakes.

Poor old Miss Easer

When I was a little girl, there was an old man in my hometown who was very odd. He and his cat slept in an old station wagon full of newspapers and odds and ends. He always kept the car in the parking spot beside his old dilapidated house. The old guy didn't live in his house because it, like his car, was stuffed with old newspapers. I was always afraid of the old man even though he had done me no harm. He just didn't look and act quite right in my childish estimation. When his old house caught fire, the police and fire company found that between the sheets of newspaper there were single dollar bills. They got bundles of the money out before the fire took it all. There are folks who feel that they must hoard all they have. The strange story of Miss Easer is one of those tales.

When eighty-two year old Miss Easer refused to pay her electricity bill in the winter of 1975, folks felt bad for her. The company, though, shut off her power and the old woman suffered in silence. However, on January 19, 1976, neighbors found her frozen body in her house. When the police arrived, they called her family in and, to everyone's amazement, Miss Easer's house in Munhall was actually a treasure trove. Shoved in closets, boxes and in various other hidey holes was over two hundred ninety-two thousand dollars in securities, cash and jewelry. The old woman was rich, but she chose to risk freezing to death rather than paying for electricity. She simply seemed unable to part with her cache.

Unlikely Gold Chest

A construction worker named Bill Bracey was working on a demolition project in Philadelphia in 1956 where he was cutting old sewer pipes. Much to his shock, he found an old section of sewer pipe filled with twenty dollar gold pieces. In fact, there was actually five thousand five hundred fifty-four dollars in gold coins in the pipe. It was certainly an unlikely repository for gold, but an amazing find none the less.

A Strange Treasure

A treasure can come from just about anywhere, and it may not be something that you were even hoping to find. Accidentally found treasures are quite common, and this one is interesting on so many levels. In 1969, a utility crew in Venango County accidentally dug up an old coffee can filled with over a hundred dollars worth of Indian head pennies. The crew was laying power lines into an old homestead for the first time when they made their unlikely find. Presumably the home owner benefited from this unexpected treasure in their own front yard.

117

PENNSYLVANIA GEMS

When people think of finding gems, they envision exotic locals such as African diamond mines or even chipping emeralds from the mountains in the western states, but Pennsylvania does have places where gems can be found. This is certainly not a complete listing, but I hope that the following will serve to pique the interest of those seriously interested in gemology. There are entire books devoted to mining, prospecting and searching for gems and minerals. Pennsylvania is not known for its gold and silver production, but it has a rich history of other gems.

Fresh Water Pearls

Aughwick Creek:

Aughwick Creek runs throughout Huntingdon County, and it is known that fresh water pearls have been found across the length of it.

Juniata River:

In Juniata County, fresh water pearls have been found along the banks of the Juniata River. Logically, though, there is a possibility of such pearls being found elsewhere along the Juniata, as well.

Semi-precious Stones

Wissahickon Garnets:

Wissahickon Valley is threaded with the beautiful semi-precious stones known as garnets. There are several sites where you might look for them. Go to the Valley Green Inn and look for the bridge that crosses the stream not far from the lot. Go up the path to the wooden shelter. Across from the shelter on the bluff you'll find what is known as Wissahickon schist or Wissahickon garnets. The stones are all along the bluff both at the top and bottom. They will not have the beautiful red color of a garnet, but if they are tumbled by a gem expert and polished they will be very beautiful. It is a unique experience and one that can be very rewarding.

You can also find the gems at a site on Bell's Mill Road. Look for the parking lots (there will be two, one on each side and a little apart from each other) and park. Walk along the creek in this area and look for river garnets. You can find these at many of the small tributaries in the area as well.

Active Gem Mines

Crystal Point Diamond Mine:

Located in Williamsport is a wonderful crystal mine that allows both novices and experts the chance to unearth some lovely stones. For a fee, the owners of Crystal Point Diamond Mine allow rock hunters a chance to dig for several types of quartz. You'll find strawberry quartz (quartz spotted with hematite), smoky quartz and black quartz along with amber quartz. Check with the mine before going. You'll also have to bring your own tools including a garden claw, screwdriver, bucket, and newspaper to wrap up the quartz so that it doesn't get damaged in transport. You can also purchase other beautiful specimens from the owners.

Gem Areas:

It is not well-known, but Delaware County is one of the best places in Pennsylvania to find gem-quality rubies and sapphires. Semi-precious gems such as quartz garnet, beryl and amethyst are also found in this county.

Lost Mines

Bear Rock Jasper Mine:

There seems to be some disagreement upon whether Bear Rock Jasper Mine existed in Northampton County, but the old stories remain. According to the tales, near Hexicoff Hill outside of Raubville there was an Indian jasper mine in the early 1700's. There is anecdotal evidence that jasper was mined in the area in the form of native jewelry and arrow points found from time to time. There are no known areas called Bear Rock today, but that doesn't mean that there never was. Take a look at a map from the 1700's, and compare it to today's maps. Many of the old names and markings no longer exist. It would be an exhaustive search, but possibly worth it to find the old mine.

Lost Silver Mine:

Supposedly in the 1700's a settler found a vein of silver and lead near his cabin near Stoneville. The cabin was said to be located at the meeting point of the Little Clearfield Creek and Morgan Run. Though the settler did mine out silver from somewhere, no one else was ever able to locate the source. It is still there somewhere, but has remained lost until this day.

The Unsuccessful Gold Mine:

Merrick Jackson was amazed when he learned that the outcropping of sandstone near his home assayed out to $16 per ton in gold ore. He tried to work the outcropping but couldn't make a living at it. The mine shut down and laid fallow until 1938 when a mining company bought it. They couldn't make a go of it either and shut it down. The mine was abandoned. The mine is located south of Coudersport and with today's refined methods it might be worth looking into again.

The Undiscovered Gold:

In Colonial times there was a story in Dauphin County that a vein of quartz was found that contained traces of gold. At the time the technology was not available to profitably mine the vein out, but today that could be possible. The site of the gold mine is said to be west of Nyes Road and where it crosses with an area south of Devonshire Road. It is rumored that silver was also located in the same area. If there is any truth to this tale, it might be worth looking into.

Here is some valuable information that could make your treasure hunting both safer and more pleasant.

Federal Parks:

Most federal parks do not allow metal detecting or treasure hunting on their land. Places such as Gettysburg and Valley Forge certainly could offer up a mountain of valuable relics, but the land is considered sacred by many. If you have any doubts, then go to the headquarters of the National Park before going out and check with them.

State Parks:

The superintendent of each park has the discretion to grant the privilege to use metal detectors. If you are planning to go to a specific park, contact them well in advance and speak to the superintendent. Be clear and honest with them about what you are doing. You may have to get a permit or fill out paperwork so you will want that done well before your arrival if possible. You can find the number for the state park that you want to visit on the Pennsylvania State Parks website.

County Parks:

These parks function under rules similar to the State Parks. Contact the director at the county park and find out what their individual rules are. If you are allowed to use metal detectors, then you will probably have to fill out a permit or other paperwork before going out.

State Forest Land:

The Pennsylvania State Department of Forestry states that it is up to the district supervisors to set the rules for metal detector usage on State Land. One of the primary concerns of district managers is where you plan to go and if it is an historic or environmentally sensitive area. Each request is weighed individually.

Water Rights:

If you decide to dive for buried treasure, property rights and water rights do apply. You will have to speak to property owners about creeks, and streams. On larger bodies of water such as Lake Erie, you might want to check with the Coast Guard before setting out. They can inform you of current rules and policies that you might need to know about. The United States Government has laid claim to many of the ship wrecks out there today. They have made it a crime to disturb them in any way. The Coast Guard also be able to provide you with or tell you where to obtain topographical underwater maps that can help you in your search. For man-made lakes in the state, you will have to check with the park that it is located in. The man-made lakes in Pennsylvania were built upon land that could have contained treasure before the flooding. Now getting to that treasure will present a different and difficult set of challenges. First get all clearances from the Park Supervisor before considering such dives.

Private Land:

Common sense rules should apply here. If you don't have the permission of the owner of the property in writing, then you could be charged with trespass. Make sure that you and property owner are clear on who will own whatever you might find. Having all of this down in writing might seem like overkill, but if you do find something it could save legal battles down the road.

COMMON SENSE RULES

Buddy System:

Using the buddy system has saved many lives throughout the years. The very nature of treasure hunting leads a person to uninhabited and potentially dangerous land. Old abandoned wells, basements and septic holes are only a few of the hazards faced by those traipsing through area where ghost towns or old farms might have been. There are also hazards brought on by wild animals and the elements to contend with. Even if you have a cell phone, you might not have coverage in the area where you get hurt. Don't count on Onstar and such things to always help you out either. I've often gone off grid in my own traipsing and startled a good friend when she went back on line with Onstar and they called her to ask her where she had been that they couldn't find her. There is nothing in this world that can replace a good buddy if you get hurt.

Tell A Friend:

Even if you and a buddy are going out to look around, don't assume that you're totally safe. Let others know where you are going and when you expect to be back. Leave a map with the area where you'll be marked on it if possible. If you change course and contact someone, let them know, too. It sounds silly in a well-populated state like Pennsylvania, but it could save a life. A few years ago, a car going down Route 30 only about a mile and a half from Breezewood went off the road, over the side of a steep mountain. It was several days before the car was found. The person was in a populated area, but there was no tree damage to indicate where the car left the road and frantic searchers took days to find the car. The person survived and was quite lucky to be alive, and that was just outside of a very high traffic area!

Do Your Homework:

If you decide to go after a specific treasure or are working a specific area, then do your homework about it. Study local maps until you are sure of the topography of the area and the hazards that you might encounter. Walk it carefully in the daytime and get your bearings. Take a compass (and know how to use it) so that you can figure out where home is if you do get lost.

If you do get lost, then a GPS can help, but it can be expensive. If you do get lost, remember to use common sense. Follow water downward and it should lead to civilization eventually. Train tracks are also good indicators of human habitation, but do be careful because if the tracks are still being used then trains will be coming. Climbing a hill could help you get your bearings so take the time. You'll have better luck with cell phone reception atop a hill, too.

If you are going with a buddy and are using two-way radios, remember that the 10 mile range advertised on the box is probably what is known as "line of sight" range. This means that if you have ten miles of uninterrupted land without mountains, houses etc. the signal will range out up to ten miles. Mountains can vastly reduce the signal range. Test your equipment before going out to be sure of its capabilities before your life could depend on it.

Be Prepared:

The old Boy Scout motto is really a good one. Every year you hear a story or two about people who got lost and died because they were unprepared. I will never forget the young couple in the Northern California Mountains who decided to take a scenic shortcut to visit family over the holidays. Unfortunately, a snowstorm stopped them and they ended up having to walk with a baby. They were totally unprepared and the mother died trying to keep her child alive. An extreme case, yes, but it could have turned out much differently if they had been prepared for it. Friends laugh because I keep bottled water, water-proof matches, blankets and other supplies in my car at all times. Have I ever needed them? Yes, once and I was prepared. My car broke down on a remote road and I had my two small sons with me. It was winter and we would have had a very rough time if not for the supplies. I made a picnic out of the dried food, we joked about going camping and I kept them warm under those blankets until help arrived. It wasn't bad at all, but then I was prepared. So keep extra water, food, etc. in the car. But don't forget to take water along with you walking. You can live quite a while without food, but water is very important. You can also get water purification tablets that will kill potentially deadly bacteria in water and pocket some of those. It might seem silly, but if you don't have them and do need them, you'll never forgive yourself. So be prepared is a great motto. And don't forget a good first aid kit!

Good luck on your treasure hunting!

Patty A. Wilson

Made in the USA
Charleston, SC
28 July 2016